ARE YOU READY FOR THE
NEW JERUSALEM

REV. FELICIA S. GAMBRAH

authorHOUSE®

AuthorHouse™
1663 Liberty Drive
Bloomington, IN 47403
www.authorhouse.com
Phone: 1 (800) 839-8640

Published by AuthorHouse 07/28/2016

ISBN: 978-1-5049-8286-3 (sc)
ISBN: 978-1-5049-8287-0 (e)

DEDICATION

This book is dedicated to my lord and savior Jesus Christ for His awesome love for mankind. Beloved let's face it, the system of this world is getting out of order. Planes, buses and trains are getting old beyond repairs. Roads and bridges are wearing out, some can't even be replaced and they are killing people in huge numbers, there is no peace amongst nations, the bible in Mathew 25:7 declares "for nations shall rise against nations and kingdoms against kingdoms: there shall be famine and pestilences and earthquakes in various Places. Even within nation, there is no peace because of wickedness and for us to know that mankind didn't evolve through monkeys and apes, but there is a true and living God who created mankind and everything the eye could see, will come back and judge the whole world because it belongs to Him. Be encouraged, get hold of the Holy Bible and read it for yourself and don't be deceived. Amen.

FOREWORD

Every now and then, the Lord touches His son or daughter to write a book that will express vision or a dream which He the Lord of glory have allowed the vessel to see His wisdom or direction for humanity. Thanks be to God for the Spirit of obedience that has quickened my daughter Pastor Gambrah to write this book the "New Jerusalem" as a metaphor for the glorious appearance of our Lord and Savior Jesus Christ.

I see the book as a wonderful expression of the love of God, the intricacies of His design for mankind to be restored to Him eternally. But most importantly, I see in New Jerusalem a demand for action on the part of believers everywhere to begin to take their rightful places as agent of preparation for entry into that Holy, eternal and most wonderful City of God. This book will challenge all followers of Christ (The Christocrats) to witness as never before in our generation. It will aggressively move us to appreciate our duties as the King's instrument of His love for the dying world that desperately need help in readying for the coming of Christ.

Presenting the message as an event that everyone must be ready for without any cost makes it effective and expectative in the heart of all reader. It is indeed an event of all history. While speaking to believers to become actively involved in preparing themselves and watching their garment less they be stained and bringing unbelievers along to the place of eternal joy. It is also persuasive enough to those who not believe or have not yet accepted Christ as their Savior to accept Him before it is too late. The expectation of a New Jerusalem coming from heaven is absolutely exciting. The joy of living and enjoying the fullness of life in the New Jerusalem cannot be negotiated because there is nothing to be compared with it. To grasped the full weight, you might want to start reading the book from chapter ten (10) as I did and the thrill, awesomeness of the King's physical presence in the Holy city is exhilarating and a great motivation to be ready to there at all cost.

But, we must not forget as the author prepared to visit the earthly Jerusalem everyone must be fully prepared. Vaccinated with the love of Christ less your bring earthly diseases and getting your approved passport signed with the blood of the King of the New Jerusalem; with these evidence of readiness, you will be fully welcomed at the port of your entry. May God bless you as you prepare for your arrival at the appointed time.

Archbishop Dr. Joseph A. Alexander
The Presiding Prelate
New Covenant Christian Ministries Worldwide
New York City

CONTENTS

PREFACE

A revelation from the Lord led me to write this book. In a dream one afternoon, I saw a multitude of people in a big boat sailing on dry ground. As it got to where I was standing, it stopped and I asked them, "Where are all of you people going?" They answered that they were the Pentecostals and were looking for the Word of God. I thought, *How can I help such uncountable people? They look pale with dry faces and almost ready to faint.* I told them I knew someone in that area who could help me assist them. As I turned, I saw that person getting ready to board a big tour bus, but she turned me down completely. She was very busy and couldn't help, because she was traveling with the people on that bus to a nearby city to purchase land to build houses. When she got on the bus, it immediately overturned, and everyone on the bus lost their right hand. When I woke up from this dream, I prayed to God for its revelation. Quickly I was led to Amos 8:11–12: "'Behold, the days are coming' says the Lord God, 'I will send a famine on the land, not a famine of bread nor a thirst for water but of hearing the words of the Lord. They shall wander from sea to sea and from north to east: They shall run to and fro, seeking the Word of the Lord but shall not find it.'"

As I was meditating on this scripture, the Lord spoke to my heart. How can people who call themselves Pentecostals be searching everywhere for the Word of God? First let's define the word *Pentecostal*:

1. Of or relating to Pentecost, a Christian festival commemorating the descent of the Holy Ghost upon the apostles.
2. Nothing or relating to any of various Christian groups, usually fundamentalist, that emphasize the activity of the Holy Spirit.

Stress holiness of living, and express their religious feelings uninhibitedly, as by speaking in tongues.

The Bible has an even more wonderful explanation in the book of Acts. So how can someone with all these experiences still be searching for the Word of God? The Bible also says in John 1:1 that in the beginning was the Word, and the Word was with God, and the Word was God.

If we did truly begin with the Word, who is Jesus, then we should be with Him every day by reading and living according to what the Word says. The Holy Spirit comes as a gift to us as we receive the Word, as at the day of Pentecost. Without the Word, our gifts can't function because the Holy Spirit is grieved by our way of life. We may operate with false gifts, but inwardly we are dry and miserable. Let's stop searching and go back to reading the Word of God, and those of us who don't have time to do God's work will lose our right hand of victory. The Holy Spirit is looking for a bride for Christ to live in the New Jerusalem—not Pentecostals or any other name we want to be called May God continue to bless you as you read this book with an open heart. Amen.

CHAPTER 1

WHO REALLY WANTS TO GO TO HEAVEN?

Lord, who shall abide in thy tabernacle?
Who shall dwell in thy holy hill? (Psalm 15:1)

The question that faced the psalmist was "Who may abide?" Too many of God's children are just content with getting to heaven, but there is much more to aim for than simply escaping hell. One of the challenges to the church in general is how to live up to the word, which tells us to abide. Who may share their life, joy, and testimonies to transform people of Christ? There is a price to pay and conditions for us to meet to be able to live up to this standard.

1. First of all, to be with God in His Holy Hill requires a new spiritual birth. John 3:1-21
2. We must walk uprightly before Him, like He told Abraham in Genesis 17:1.
3. We must speak the truth in our hearts. Being honest with others is impossible if we are not honest with ourselves in our hearts.
4. We shouldn't talk against one another in any way that is destructive, malicious, or unkind, even if it's the truth. Let's examine our motives before we talk about anyone. If our hearts are pure, our lips will be pure.
5. If we appreciate unbelievers and enjoy their company, those whose hearts are not pure and who don't live in a holy manner,

how then shall we enjoy the company of those who shall be the inhabitants of the high and holy place spending eternity in high places?

6. We must honor those who fear God. They are our family, no matter where they live or what are their positions in life.

7. We shouldn't make vows that we definitely know we can't honor. A broken vow reveals weakness of character.

8. We shouldn't lend to a brother or a sister and then demand that he or she give back more than we lent.

If we do these things, no one shall be able to evict us out of God's holy hill. We shall dwell there with Him forever in the New Jerusalem. No matter how we assess our church or our Christian life, none of us can get things right unless the church is led by the Holy Spirit.

David made God his all, so God chose an inheritance for David by giving him many blessings. Yet David hungered for more because the grass looked greener on the other side. Nevertheless, what David did could not destroy God's promise of the Messiah through his inheritance. God forgave David when he repented, though he paid a high price for what he did. He made God his shepherd and his all because true love does not record wrong but instead covers wrongs. Our God is so merciful. God dealt leniently with David and spared his life.

I don't know how people can live without Him. We should fear Him and serve Him with a grateful heart. Think about His greatness, His creation. When you fly in an airplane and look down on the clouds and see their beautiful design, you realize how awesome God is. And looking down, you will also see mountains, forests, deserts, seas, and many wonderful things that reveal the greatness and power of God. Yet He sent His son in the form of man to be born here. He died to redeem mankind. If truly God is your shepherd, you will not lack anything, and His goodness will come toward you. He will make sure you get your daily bread, He will bless your drinking water, He will restore your soul with His salvation, and His Holy Spirit will help you to live a holy and purified life. Yes, you will always feel His presence, no matter how deep your valley or how high your mountain of adversity. He will promote and strengthen you by empowering you you with an overflow of blessing and goodwill. In this life and forever, He will preserve you in His house as He prepares you for the New Jerusalem, our chief joy. And while He is doing this, He will make sure your enemies see His saving hand upon your life. They will be put to shame, and His name will be glorified in the end.

But if we call ourselves His children and are not dedicated to Him fully, we will lack the true joy that comes with our salvation. We will always lack true inner peace. People around us will wonder whether God is our true shepherd. We will be looking for green pastures while He leads His sheep to the green pastures because He knows where the green pastures are. Fear will always be in our hearts, and we will never be satisfied in our faith. We may be sheep, but He can never be our shepherd because most of the time we are following the voice of a stranger who is always leading us astray. Our enemies are always planning evil against us, throwing us into valleys of deadly shadows, and piercing us with fake joy and prosperity, things that do not last.

The psalmist asked the Lord a question after walking after the heart of God and knowing who He was. He asked how any man can live with such a God in this holy heaven. But thanks be to our Lord and Savior Jesus Christ, who came and paved the highway with His own blood. Now those who want to go are following His footsteps with their new heart, wearing white robes, their names written in the Lamb's book of life. The spirit of wisdom and revelation has revealed to them that this world is not their home. They would rather be a doorkeeper in the house of their God than dwell in the tents of wickedness. In these end times, there are many tents of wickedness. Because we don't love one another deeply in the Lord, our Christian gatherings and our homes become tents of wickedness. If the flat-screen TV in your house is on twenty-four hours a day, if you watch movies instead of spending time with the Lord, if you're always on the phone with your friends and not respecting the presence of the Lord—beware, child of God. You are turning your home into a tent of wickedness with no peace or rest. The atmosphere is tense because the glory of the Lord has departed. Those who want to be with the Lord on the holy hill are always ready because no one knows the hour of His coming or the hour of our departure from this life. The devil will intentionally keep you busy.

Here is the answer to the question the Psalms ask: "He who walks uprightly and works righteousness and speaks the truth in his heart" (Psalm 15:2). He who created mankind and this world knows perfectly that, after the fall of man in the Garden of Eden, another salvation plan must be made to redeem man back to God. That is the depth of God's goodness and love. Because man cannot work for his own righteousness and uprightness, man's own way of obtaining salvation through his own goodness will be useless. The Word of God clearly says that "all our righteous deeds are like filthy rags" (Isaiah 64:6).

When we go out to evangelize, some of the people we talk to have this idea that they are not living in sin. I spoke to one person who said, "I am holy because, since my husband died, I live by myself. I don't go out to bars anymore. I don't gossip, I don't curse, I love everybody, I speak to everyone nicely, and I don't lie." In other words, she doesn't need to be bothered with Jesus and this salvation thing. She even said she goes to church, once in a while reads the book of Psalms, and say her prayers every day. I think these are the ideas that the devil uses to block people's minds to the truth of their need for salvation. But according to the Bible, all these acts are like filthy rags.

At least Nicodemus made an effort by going to Jesus to inquire more about salvation, fascinated by the miracles as described in John 3. But Jesus, being God and filled with the Holy Ghost, and knowing the real reason why Nicodemus was there, went straight to the point. Nicodemus was a Pharisee and a ruler who wanted something more than the religious rituals he had been performing. Jesus assured Nicodemus that he needed a new birth, a spiritual birth, which only Christ can give if we will believe in Him, accept Him, and obey His teachings. The Holy Spirit will come and dwell in us, to help us lead a Christian life that will lead us to see the kingdom of God. Our names will be in God's book of life, and heaven will be our eternal home.

Well, maybe you are reading this book and saying to yourself, *How can this be?* But I encourage you to accept Christ because Jesus was born and died at the cross to reconcile man back to God. See what a wonderful father you will have! Dear fellow kingdom workers, I want to encourage all of us. In the course of this work, and as we see the unfolding events around the globe, some people will come to us, like Nicodemus, to inquire about our faith and hope. With love, try to present Christ to them. Show them their need for a Savior as we reason with them through the scriptures. We need to study and show ourselves approved, as Paul admonishes Timothy, by rightfully sharing this truth with them. We don't want people's blood on our hands. We don't want people going to hell, for no one can live a righteous life without accepting Jesus Christ or speaking the truth from their heart.

The Psalms warn us not to backbite with our tongues. James 3:6–12 says that the tongue is a fire, a world of iniquity that can destroy and defile our whole body. The smallest among our body parts, the tongue can set hellfire because it carries the power of life and death. As members of Christ's body, we are not to destroy our brother. With our tongues, we are destroying ourselves. If we wish someone dead, we will die first because we are carrying this thought in our heart. The lack of love among ourselves causes all kind of troubles. As Christians, prayer is our nutrition that we feed on to survive and communicate with our father. If evil words come out of our mouths, we are not holy. Then I don't think God hears us, because the Holy Spirit in us is grieved. But if we yield to the Holy Spirit one more time, His fruits will be released: joy, love, patience, and all those good things will come into our new hearts. Then a new tongue will be installed and our prayers will be answered. Free access will be granted to us by His grace, to be with Him on His holy hill, the New Jerusalem.

We should share each other's burdens. Christ didn't seek His own. He died a crucifixion death, a blood-drained death, for His blood to reach all nations. If we dislike one another, we may certainly gossip and backbite. But the Lord commands us to love our enemies and leave the revenge to Him. Some of us came to Christ through pain and disgrace, and we promise to serve Him with all our heart and everything we have. But going down the line, we become proud and can't even give our brother a ride home after church. We swear in our own hearts, but now we have changed drastically. We serve God on our own terms, choosing whom we want to greet and talk to. This shouldn't be. If you lend money to your brother, don't overcharge the interest. God doesn't want us to do that. Instead, seek heavenly interest.

Taking a Bribe Against the Innocent

There is nothing new under the sun. Nothing is a surprise to God. You may wonder, *How can the person who claims to love God or calls himself a child of God give or accept bribes?* Okay, I want us to be aware of what Judas Iscariot did. We all know how, as described in Matthew 26 and 27, Judas became jealous of his master and betrayed Jesus for thirty pieces of silver. Judas himself said, "I have sinned by betraying innocent blood." The chief priest didn't put the money in their treasury, because to them it was blood money.

In the same manner, Joseph's brothers, as described in Genesis 37, sold him for twenty shekels. Yes, a servant is not greater than his master. Judas betrayed Jesus for thirty pieces of silver, not shekels. Joseph's brothers betrayed him for twenty shekels. But in the end, Judas died before Jesus, and Joseph's brothers bowed down to him. Beloved, there are certain characteristics that will never grant us access to dwell with the Lord on His holy hill. Maybe you say, "Oh, I can never do that." But in so many ways, we betray our Lord Jesus Christ by hiding behind His name, defrauding people through false prophecies and so forth, not realizing the times and the season we live in during this twenty first century.

We betray one another when we don't seek the good and the welfare of our brother. It may look like you are the only one God loves and talks to, and that everyone should join your church if they want to live in a good way. But you never support or pray for your brother's ministry. Cain killed his brother Abel, as described in Genesis 4, because of jealousy. When God asked Cain about his brother, he became angry and said, "I don't know." He even asked God, "Am I my brother's keeper?" As one preacher said, if we are not our brothers' keepers, then we break fellowship with one another. Because of our lack of love for one another, we betray one another. We seek to hear bad news about one another, not even taking time to call and encourage each other, but rather spreading rumors. Gossip is even worse than taking a bribe because what you heard may not be true.

I wonder what has happened to the blood that bought the church of Jesus Christ. What did we do with the love of God that we received when He came to dwell in us? Let us return to our first love. We can't continue to preach all these unsearchable riches of Christ while losing sight of the main point: love God and love your brother, for love is God. Beloved, we can never be moved if we go by these lines, and God's holy hill will be our eternal home. The devil tries to shift our focus to bad relationships and life issues to lower our self-esteem and to secretly drive us into the flesh. Psalm 4:7 tells us that the Lord can put joy in the hearts of His children. That's why we always have to keep our hearts pure, even loving our enemies.

There are so many things the Lord wants to do in our lives. He wants to reside there, to be the center of our joy. He wants to commune with us to make the relationship strong, pleading our cause. He wants to fight the battles that are beyond our ability to control, which often rob us of our joy. Also, we don't normally know all the strategies of the devil or his battle plan, unless the Holy Spirit leads us. Therefore we must offer God worship and praise, and not entertain fear in ourselves in this life. Our focus should always be on how we are going to live with our God in His holy heaven to have inner joy. People may congratulate you for achievement, but that will not save your soul. People in Hollywood do not live in apartments or houses—they live in mansions, to demonstrate the power of their wealth. Our Lord has promised us heavenly mansions, and can you imagine what that's going to be like? This should put joy in your heart. Sometimes we read the scriptures and God's promises seem like fairy tales. But we must keep our fire burning because soon and very soon we will be going to meet our king. To continue be an everlasting child of God, we must be encouraged.

The world we live in now is engaged in a terrible warfare, and the key to victory is in the hands of the church. In Deuteronomy 20, Moses encourages the children of Israel to disregard what they see and hear—the threat of the enemy who wants to terrorize them with war. The arm of God that brought them out of Egypt is strong to deliver, even more so today, for anyone who will put his trust in this living God and vow to serve Him. We must continue to keep our fire burning.

Most of us who have had the opportunity to walk with God for a while can testify that nothing we build our joy around can fulfill our hearts' desires. The Holy Spirit leads me into this truth. I once considered myself to be a defeated Christian, not knowing that He had already fulfilled it. Joy does not come with materialism, but with satisfaction of the soul. The joy that comes in this life can't give me satisfaction. So as believers, we should not open ourselves up for all kinds of deceit. There are scriptures in the Bible that plainly explain the characteristics of those who don't want to abide in God's tabernacle. In Galatians 5:19, the works of the sinful nature are clearly explained:

1. Adultery—voluntary sexual intercourse between a married person and a person who is not his or her spouse
2. Fornication—sexual intercourse between people not married to each other
3. Uncleanness—being dirty or filthy in body and soul
4. Lewdness—being very sexual or lustful in an offensive way

5. Idolatry—making things, including ourselves, into a god
6. Sorcery—the use of magic, especially black magic
7. Hatred—intense dislike or ill will
8. Contention—heated disagreement
9. Jealousy—the state or feeling of being jealous
10. Outburst of wrath—a violent moment that carries the face of wrath
11. Selfish ambition—an intense drive for success
12. Dissension—standing apart
13. Heresy—an opinion or doctrine contrary to the original truth
14. Envy—coveting another's advantages and success
15. Murder—unlawful killing and abortion
16. Drunkenness—excessive intake of alcohol leading to a breakdown
17. Revelry—noisy partying or a merrymaking way of life

Nothing associated with these works is acceptable for a Holy Ghost believer.

This list is followed with a clear warning that people who practice such things will never inherit the kingdom of God. As a believer, you've vowed to stay holy and live your life till death. But what about jealousy and anger, those unseen sins? Let's pray and get rid of them, so that we can tabernacle with the Lord. Let's look at another signboard. But cowards, unbelievers, murderers, sexually immoral, sorcerers, idolaters, and liars shall have their part in the lake that burns with fire and brimstone, which is the second death. In Luke 21–8, we can also read about the works of the flesh, especially sexual immorality. That's why pornography is now an epidemic everywhere. However, we are being warned here that as born-again children of God, this should never be said about us. I know people will still want to have it both ways, but that can never happen with God. If we are still struggling with these fleshly desires, there is always grace for us to ask God to forgive us and cleanse us from all unrighteousness. We must do so if we want to tabernacle with God on His holy hill, the New Jerusalem, rather than spend eternity with Satan in the lake of fire and brimstone.

Why would you choose a lake of fire instead of a golden street? Let's ponder these choices because we will definitely have to make a choice. God always wants the best for His children, and we should always work out our salvation with fear. Some of us have sworn in our heart to be faithful to God, but still with a divided heart we are strong in the Lord only halfway. Even the remaining 50 percent is not all for the Lord. What a pity! Some of us respect what Hollywood actors say and do more than what we hear from our pastors and the Word of God. If we really want to be with God, we need to live holy and righteous lives every day because tomorrow may not be ours. God told the children of Israel in Amos 5:40, "Seek me and live. Stop going to Bethel, Gilgal and Beersheba—all these sacrifice that don't please Me." For God, obedience is always better than sacrifice. After the sheep and the ox, you are not talking to your wife. You are organizing a marriage seminar. Why don't we always judge ourselves first and see whether we are in the faith, before doing all these camouflaging things? Are we still serving this holy God or not? Do we really want to be with Him in eternity, or are we just playing games to please people and church members? Let us answer for ourselves. Hebrews 1:1–2 says that in times past, God used to talk to His people through the prophets. But in these last days, He has spoken to us through His son Jesus Christ, not through the words of good or bad prophets. The words of Christ should dwell in us richly, although He still speaks through His end-time prophets.

In Acts 28:31, the apostle Paul says, "Preaching the Kingdom of God and teaching the things which concern the Lord Jesus Christ with all confidence, no one forbidding him." If we really want to be His true heavenly bound children, we must preach about His second coming and the kingdom of God, so that the gates of hell cannot even come close to destroy His church and people.

CHAPTER 2

JERUSALEM ON EARTH

❦

As a child, I used to hear the word *Jerusalem* only in songs. When I grew up, I heard it in Bible readings at church and later discovered that there is a place called *Jerusalem* here on earth. I became excited and decided to visit there someday.

Thanks be to God the father for giving us His only begotten son, whose blood is able to save every soul in this universe. After I had been saved and received forgiveness through Jesus's blood, He sealed me with the Holy Spirit of promise. When I discovered in the Bible that there is a new spiritual Jerusalem above, for every truly repented, born-again child of God filled with His spirit, and that we will have a final destination and home in this New Jerusalem, my desire to visit the Jerusalem on earth intensified.

Years back, when the Lord put it in my spirit to write this book (I can't even remember the exact year), I knew that for me to understand the subject of this book, I had to make a trip to Israel. But that idea seemed impossible to me, so I shut the idea of writing this book out of my mind.

Satan was happy. He bombarded me with laziness and all sorts of excuses. Then the Holy Spirit came in mightily with the sword. "I can do all things through Christ which strengthens me" (Philippians 4:13). If it's true that our being and existence is from Him, then we have access to everything. Anytime we disassociate ourselves from God's

Word, we become hopeless and useless—like trodden salt, good for nothing concerning the kingdom and our secular business.

The New Jerusalem is the future everlasting home for all believers. Most of us are more comfortable and excited in our earthly homes and apartments than in the prepared and adorned one from our father. "Let not your heart be troubled, ye believe in God, believe also in Me. In my father's house are many mansions. If it were not so, I would not have told you I go to prepare a place for you" (John 14:1–2).

It's my prayer that every child of God will be able to visit Israel once in his or her lifetime. Of course that will not guarantee access to heaven, but for the love of Christ and the Jewish people. Many people have visited Israel, and some have even lived there for a variety of reasons. But for the first time Spirit-filled believer, it is a remarkable spiritual journey.

I took a connecting flight from New York to Atlanta, and then traveled with the group to Tel Aviv. I waited for about six hours before our departure. Most of the women in the group had visited Israel many times, but this was my first trip. I just wanted to go to Israel. It was everything I had been praying about, and the trip was very emotional for me. We were given a list of things we should bring. I didn't want to be disobedient in any way concerning this trip, so I had everything on the list.

When I told my Archbishop Joseph Alexander, a man who has a Christocracy vision around the world about my trip, he was very excited and said, "Oh, my daughter, you are going to walk in the master's footprints. May God be with you on your journey." That was all I needed to hear from a man filled with the Holy Spirit and wisdom.

I had forgotten to take an alarm clock, but on my arrival at the Atlanta airport, American Express was doing a promotion for people to sign up and receive gift items, including alarm clocks. So I signed up quickly to receive a free alarm clock. Indeed, the Lord will supply all our needs— and sometimes, even our wants. He loves us so much, especially if we obey Him as we should.

When we receive the Lord as our Savior, we should receive everything about Him joyfully. Going to Israel was not just another trip to satisfy my curiosity. It was for the love of my Savior, Jesus and what He has done for all of us.

It was a long flight. On the plane, I saw some rabbis nodding their heads in prayer, so I left the prayer part to them. I knew definitely that I was on my way to Israel, and I was careless about what would happen to the plane. It was all part of my excitement. I said, "Lord, dead or alive, it's all for your glory."

The flight was very smooth. As they announced that we would soon be landing at Tel Aviv's Ben Gurion Airport, it was 6:00 p.m. Middle East time. I thought it was morning because I had slept throughout the flight, but they served us pizza. I was wondering if that was for breakfast. I heard two guys in front of me talking about it, too. One of them was also asking his friend why Israel served pizza for breakfast. He also thought it was morning.

By the time we drove from Tel Aviv to Jerusalem, it was foggy outside. I didn't quite remember the time, because the bus was delayed at the airport. As it was announced that we were entering Jerusalem, I stretched my neck to look at the mountains, but I couldn't see them very well. I was thinking about Jesus and how his enemies wanted to throw Him off a high cliff. Scriptures were just running through my mind. I was talking to myself in prayer, telling the Lord how sorry I was for Him going through all that just to reconcile sinners to His father. I used to be one of those sinners back then.

Finally, we were able to get to our hotel. My roommate was already in bed, so I couldn't talk much. The next morning, I looked through the window at the city. I sang songs of praise to God for bringing me to Israel and for blessing Jerusalem. Indeed, the children of Israel have been scattered all around the world, but by God's mercy and the promise to bring them back to their own land, God has fulfilled His promise. "Then the Lord will scatter you among all nations, from one end of the earth to the other. There you will worship other gods—gods of wood and stone, which neither you nor your ancestors have known" (Deuteronomy 28:64).

Isaiah 11:11 says, "In that day The Lord shall set his hand again the second time time and recover the Remnant of his people, who shall be left, from Assyria from Egypt, from pathros, from cush from hamath and from the islands of the sea." According to biblical history, Cush is modern-day Ethiopia. I saw black children going to school, and I was told they were the Ethiopian Jews who had come back to their roots. They seemed so happy. They were officially recognized by the state of Israel in 1973.

The restoration of Jerusalem is an important fulfillment of the last days' prophecy, to which many Christians are not paying attention. This includes the Messianic Jewish movement. The Messianic Jews are coming to Christ as their Savior by faith. And the lost Jewish tribes are gathering, such as the Ethiopians, the Pashtun of Afghanistan, the Ibis of Nigeria, the Bnet of India, the Lemma of Zimbabwe, and many more. These signs should wake the church up in preparation to meet our Savior. Let's pay close attention to the nation of Israel as the last days are coming nearer.

The day before our departure, a guy who traveled with our group had a visitation. The Lord appeared in his room and said with a loud voice, "My name is Yeshua." As a matter of fact, this guy didn't want to go to Israel, but his mother had encouraged him to go. As he was debating with himself whether to take this trip or not, all of a sudden a brighter light flashed in his room and a loud voice spoke. Shaken by this revelation, he immediately packed his suitcase and was at the airport before everyone else.

When he shared this testimony, every one of us was trying to find out what else Jesus said. Was it just "My name is Yeshua"? We were wondering why Jesus would identify Himself with His Messianic name to someone who was not even willing to take a holy trip to Israel for the sake of his loving Savior.

The Messianic Jews who believe that Jesus is the Messiah call Him Yeshua. The Hebrew name Yeshua is the Jewish name that Jesus would have been called by those who knew Him. Some Messianic and other groups say Yeshua is Jesus's real name, but to those of us saved by His blood, His name is uncountable.

The name Jesus did more wonders than the master Himself. Unto all of us who came to be saved and baptized into this great name, if He wants us to call Him Yeshua, it shouldn't be a debatable issue at all. That's why all roads lead to Israel, for the king is coming. That's why He is identifying with His people by introducing Himself with the name

Yeshua. It won't be long before we will be with our Savior. He loves the Jewish people and loves us all, too. What a Savior!

The Israeli Army

I saw young men and women in military uniforms everywhere we went. The scripture that came to my mind was Matthew 11:12: "And from the days of John the Baptist until now, the Kingdom of heaven suffereth violence, and men of violence take it by force." They are the army of violence. They need to protect their nation and their people because the enemy always wants to swallow them up. So it is with us, the New Testament church. We must be vigilant, for the kingdom we are seeking is not a summer picnic. We must always be ready, putting on the whole armor of God because the warfare is very real.

While in Hebron, we got off the buses to make a declaration over the city. By the time we turned back, we didn't hear armored cars coming, but we were surrounded by their army. They knew we were coming to that site, yet they needed to come and check on us to see if we were what we said we were. I felt very secure.

I also learned that Israel's military forces include ground forces, air force, and navy—the IDF, or Israel Defense Force. The number of wars and border conflicts in which the IDF has been involved make their army one of the most battle-trained armed forces in the world, from the Old Testament era to this present age. There is a lesson to be learned here. Child of God, the battle never ends, so get up and dress in your spiritual armor and fight the good fight of faith, for this God of Israel is our God.

The Promised Land

Modern-day Israel is called the Promised Land. Its history began when God called Abraham to leave his homeland and go to a new land, which God was going to show him, called Canaan: "Get out of your country, from your family, and from your father's house to a land that I will show you" (Genesis 12:1).

This is the land known as Israel, named after Abraham's grandson Jacob. God changed Jacob's name to Israel when he had an encounter with the angel of God. His descendants are the Jewish people who now live in modern Israel, people who don't know what the Bible says about this promise. For over 3,200 years, since the conquest of Joshua, the Jews have lived in this land continuously, although they have not always been in political control of the land. The land of Israel now is central to Judaism: "But I say to you, you shall possess their land; and I will give it to you as an inheritance, a land flowing with milk and honey, I am the Lord your God, who has set you apart from the nations" This calls for literal warfare, so don't be surprised by what you see and hear. The Talmud says the land is so holy that merely walking in it can gain you a place in the coming world. I was very careful walking in the streets of Jerusalem not to drop even a candy wrapper. I saw cigarette stubs and other trash, just like in any city. But my mind was on Christ Jesus my Lord, whose spiritual and physical origins were in this holy land. The land was not handed to Israel on a silver platter. God has commanded them to dispossess and possess it, and by their vigilance and militant spirit, they have possessed the land until now. God is continually blessing them despite the opposition they face daily.

His promises are yes and amen to His glory. For those of us who are seeking the second appearance of Christ, our redeemer knows for sure that whatever the father has promised through His son Jesus Christ will surely come to pass. God's promise to Abraham has been fulfilled and Israel has become a nation, so His promise to take us to the New Jerusalem will surely take place. We live now in daily preparation for Christ's second coming as we proclaim the gospel wherever we go through the wisdom of the Holy Ghost. Israel is our evidence that every word of God is sure, and that's why it is impossible for the prince of this world to overthrow the church of Christ and His people. We must fight a good fight of faith and possess the inheritance the Lord has given us. Even in this land of the living, poverty, sickness, rejection, and all the goods of the devil can never destroy us because the earth is the Lord's and the fullness thereof. We must prosper and live well, so as to continue the good work by sharing the love of God with others.

We had checked in at Tel Aviv's Ben Gurion International Airport on our way home from Israel when I saw people moving fast to a certain location. One woman claimed to have seen a big, unidentified black bag, thereby spreading fear all over, but the whole ten days I spent in Israel was the most peaceful time in my entire life. I kept postponing going to Israel because of what I saw and heard in the news, but I came back fearless. Beloved, God still watches over His Word to perform it, and in these days of terrorism, our only hope and shield is in Jehovah. "Thou will keep him in perfect peace, whose mind is stayed on thee; because he trusts in thee." Isaiah 26:3

The nation of Israel trusted the God who promised their fathers—Abraham, Isaac, and Jacob—to give them this land as their inheritance, and they still trust Him for their protection. We need the mind of Christ to live our daily lives because He is the prince of peace and our protection is guaranteed. You can't be depressed when you think about heaven and the love of God, the things He has prepared for those who love Him.

The Garden Tomb

To begin our sightseeing, we first visited the garden tomb, which is near the heart of Jerusalem. The most important thing I really wanted to see was the empty tomb there in the garden. We took Holy Communion, which gave us the energy and the spiritual boost we needed to cover all the sites in ten days. Groups of people from other nations were there. Some men were lying on the floor crying like babies, and it was very emotional. Others conducted a memorial service by singing Good Friday and Easter hymns, to show their appreciation to the Savior. Their anointing oil is very expensive, and so are photographs. I wondered whether the place still belongs to the descendants of Joseph of Arimethea, who was a secret believer in Jesus despite being a member of the Sanhedrin (Mark 15:43). He buried Jesus in his tomb because it is always good to give to the Lord.

Then we journeyed north to Shechem in biblical Samaria, where we began to retrace the promise of God's plan through His blessing to Abram. At Shechem, the Lord appeared to Abram and said, "To your descendants I will give this land," and it was here that Abraham built his first and second altars (Genesis 12:7, 13:5). Abraham communicated with the Lord by building altars of worship. Building an altar is an intentional, physical act of worship. When Abraham returned from Egypt, he saw the altar he had originally made, and he called on the name of the Lord in thanks and adoration. We don't need to build altars, but to be as dedicated and international as Abraham in our relationship with God. We should rather build an invisible altar in our spirit, to serve God through our helper, the Holy Spirit. Altars are still regarded as holy places in our sanctuaries and must be respected. We can't kneel at our sanctuary altars and offer our petitions with an unbelieving heart. God still loves His children.

Mount Gerizim

We also stood on the high place of Mount Gerizim and recalled the blessings for obedience pronounced by Moses (Deuteronomy 2:27–28). There we prayed and interceded for the whole body of Jesus Christ to be obedient to the Holy Spirit. As we head toward the end of this age, disobedient spirits will overtake many people, by doing their own thing and stamping it with the name of the Lord. The Word of God is our guide; if it's not in the Bible, please just forget it and let's come back to the course. In this region, we learned that I was standing where Jesus spoke to the Samaritan woman when He introduced a new spiritual worship. The well is still there, and most of us picked up some stones as a memorial, praying and thanking God that we don't have to travel every year to Israel before we can worship God. For me, the journey was not easy, but I know people go there every year. Amen to that.

The next day, after our morning devotion, we called forth resurrection life outside the city walls at the garden tomb. For the nation of Israel and the body of Christ, we asked that the resurrected life of our Lord bring salvation, fruitfulness, abundant life, new authority, and new identity in the Spirit to His people. After a visit to the upper room, we went to the old city, and on the ramparts of the temple we saw Mount Moriah: "Then Solomon began to build the house of the Lord at Jerusalem in Mount Moriah, where David his father, in the place that David had prepared in the threshing floor of Ornan the Jebusite" (2 Chronicles 3:1). Mount Moriah is where Abraham almost offered Isaac as a sacrifice to God. It is also identified as the location of Aruna the Jebusite's threshing floor, which David bought for six hundred shekels of gold. That also demonstrates that the Jews received this area through a legal transaction. And for the believer who wants to live in the mansion of the father's house above, surrender and give a sacrifice that is costly. Let's give our best because Christ gave His all. We prayed, looking over the city of David, and declared that the mountain of the Lord's house shall be established on the top of the mountains. These are still prayer points for believers waiting for the second coming of Christ.

We went from Jerusalem to Shechem in biblical Samaria. There we began to retrace the promise of God's plan through His blessing to Abram, when He said, "To your descendants I will give this land."

Mount of Olives

Then we visited the mount from which Christ ascended and to which He will return. "Which also said, ye men of Galilee, why stand ye gazing up into heaven? This same Jesus, which is taken up from you into heaven, shall so come in like manner as ye have seen Him go into heaven" (Acts 1:11). Beloved, Jesus Christ will surely come back, and so with this faith we serve and worship Him faithfully.

A lot of people are gazing at anything and everything, but not at heaven. Beloved, what are you gazing at? What is taking your attention away from Jesus? What are you steadily, intently gazing at in this life? Some people can't take their eyes from their TV, or just anything that catches their eye. I once saw a man gazing at a woman like he had just dropped from the moon. He looked at her so much that even when a car horn was blowing, he couldn't hear it and almost lost his life. Many people have gazed and lost their dignity and life also, and some of God's children don't gaze at the Word anymore. They are soldiers without a sword, trying to win spiritual battles.

The apostles gazed at Jesus's disappearance. Nobody knows how long they did this before God sent ministry angels to comfort them with a promise of His reappearance in the future. They couldn't take their eyes off the master. While we were looking at the skies over Jerusalem, it started to rain. Some of us were praying for a miracle, to see Him coming on our watch. What an awesome experience that would be. He's definitely coming back, so let's get ready. It will be a great day for all who are waiting for Him.

Bethlehem

We couldn't go into Bethlehem, but we did travel to the outskirts of the city of Jesus's birth, which is now a Muslim town. We couldn't go there as we wished. But thank God, He is not coming to reclaim anything in this life except his chosen saints, after the New Jerusalem is complete, over two thousand years later. Bethlehem today is in Palestine, not Israel. So we just stood a distance away and viewed the city of our Lord's birth.

Negev

Negev, in the wilderness of Beer Sheva, covers over half of Israel's total land area. Touring in the Negev desert was amazing for those of us who hadn't ever seen a desert. It also has some interesting historical sites, such as copper mines and beautiful works of nature. We offered many prayers here for the descendants of two sons of Abraham, Isaac and Ishmael.

The church must still pray for the descendants of these two brothers (Genesis 16:9, 21:8–20). The church must still pray for Israel. God has not finished with them yet. The Word of God commands us to do so (Psalm 122:6). The church of Jesus Christ has a continuing dependency upon the past, present, and future of Israel. Our Lord is for yesterday, today, and forever. Their blindness opened our spiritual eyes, and God still loves them very dearly. He has an everlasting covenant with Abraham.

Ishmael was the first born of Abraham with Hagar. "As for Ishmael I have heard you! Behold I bless him and will make him fruitful and multiply him. He shall father twelve princes, and I will make him a great nation" (Genesis 17:20). God heard the plea of his friend Abraham and blessed the descendants of Ishmael (modern-day Muslims), which is a massive reality in our day. Our crucified, risen, and reigning Lord Jesus is ready and able to reach out to them in love, again to make it clear that God chose the line of Isaac over the line of Ishmael. God does the same thing again in Genesis 15:21, when Isaac prays and God grants them twins, Jacob and Esau. God decided that Jacob would be the line of promise and He declared, "The older shall serve the younger" (Genesis 25:23). They need our prayers, for the spirit of the boy Ishmael is still crying in the wilderness.

East Arad

East Arad is a city in the south district of Israel, on the border of the Negev and Judean deserts. That morning when we drove to Arad, I was exhausted. When I heard our tourist coach saying we were visiting the "fountain of tears," I asked my roommate if we were going to cry there, but she didn't know either. To my understanding, that's the name of the place, which has a wonderful collection of prophetic sculptures that depict the Jewish Messiah and the Holocaust Jew. Not many can imagine the suffering, but Jesus Christ was with those who suffered execution during the Holocaust. This place explains the message of the Jewish Christ's compassion and identification with His people. What I saw in this museum can't be described with words. During the Holocaust, more than six million Jews were killed in the concentration camps. The sculptures are intended to depict the seven words on the cross, and how the Messiah could identify and empathize with his Jewish people because of His own execution on the cross. No one comes out this place without tearful eyes. My fountain of tears blinded me. I couldn't find my way to the bus, and I became so sick that I had to see a doctor the next day. Dear believer, all that we go through in this Christian life will end with Shalom. Beloved, it is a sight to see. Whenever you visit Israel, you'll see that nothing can break them and nothing can break us.

Jericho

On our way to the Dead Sea, we stopped to pray at Jericho, the first city conquered by Joshua so that the Jews could enter the promised land. According to the book of Joshua, Jericho was the first battle after crossing the Jordan (Joshua 6:1–27). The walls of Jericho fell after the Israelite army marched around the city blowing their trumpets. For the children of God, the battle still rages on. Without holiness and consistent prayer, we will never get to our promised land. We stood on the grounds of Jericho and prayed that the spirit of militancy would consume the church of Jesus Christ. Beloved, prayer is a force that needs to be pushed against the kingdom of darkness.

Mount Tabor

On our way to Nazareth, we stopped at Mount Tabor, where Barak told Deborah to go to war with him (Joshua 5 and Judges 4). There we offered prayers that both men and women would be active in God's vineyard, working together as we await our Lord's coming. We always salute our men as the head because God ordained that. But please, don't dominate the women, for together the work is completely done. Recognize the Deborahs and allow them to exercise their gifts. Thank God that Barak recognized not just the prophetic mantle, but a warrior, who was much needed at that time.

Nazareth

I was happy to be in Nazareth, which is among the hills that constitute the south of Lebanon, near modern Cana. Nazareth is said in the New Testament to be the city of Jesus because He lived there during the first thirty years of His life (Matthew 2:23). Jesus visited Nazareth during his public ministry, but did not perform miracles there because of unbelievers. At the hotel room, I could hear loud Islamic songs and couldn't believe we were in Nazareth, the hometown of Jesus Christ.

Cana

In Nazareth, we visited Cana, where Jesus turned water into wine at a wedding (John 2). Wine sellers are making their fortunes at the wine stores. Some couples were blessing their marriage at a chapel, and others traveled there to have their wedding vows renewed. I pray that married couples should always stay together and drink the never-ending wine with Jesus until death parts them.

Mount Carmel

At Mount Carmel, the group agreed together to pray against all false voices and doctrines that oppose God's voice and the fulfillment of His plan (Matthew 16:18–21; 2 Chronicles 20:14–20). Most of us are aware of the dangers that false prophecy brings to a nation or an individual life, but prophecy from God edifies the church. As the end time draws nearer, we see spiritual adultery increasing in the body of Christ. False prophets will flourish as highly sought-after speakers because of the itching ears of the people (Acts 17:11). We've neglected the reading of the Bible, the most up-to-date prophetic book on Earth, to listen to the voices of men. May God forgive us. In Revelation 19:20, the false prophet, who is Satan the beast, will perform great miracles. He can even cause fire to come from heaven, and he will delude people into receiving the number of the beast (and of man), which is the number 666. People who refuse will be beheaded. Satan is subtle. He will not just say, "Here I am. Let me put a mark on your forehead." But as we continue to dabble with these false prophets, the church will be weakened and will deviate from the original order and purpose God intended for us.

There are so many sites to visit in Israel that you can't cover everything in just one visit. Oh beloved, it is my prayer that a door will be opened for you to visit the Holy Land before our Lord comes for His bride, the church of Jesus Christ.

CHAPTER 3

YOUR JEBUSITE WILL BE YOUR JERUSALEM

—————————— ❦ ——————————

Spoke unto David, saying, Except thou
Take away the blind and the lame, Thou
Shalt not come in hither. Thinking David
Cannot come in hither.

—2 Samuel 5:6

According to biblical history, the Jebusites are believed to be descendants of Canaan. They were thought to be warlike people living in the mountains. But after David became king over all Israel, he needed a good place to build his house, a place that would befit a king. He discovered that Jerusalem, where the Jebusites dwelt, would be a suitable place to build his palace and rule over Israel. The Jebusites intimidated David and insulted him, but David fought and captured this stronghold for Zion to become the city of David, the earthly Jerusalem. Beloved, David did not say, "Oh, I wish these Jebusites' land would become mine someday." He fought for and captured it.

When God revealed Himself to Moses (Exodus 3) at Mount Horeb, He instructed Moses to bring the children of God from slavery in Egypt to a land that originally belonged to the Canaanites, Hittites, Amorites, Perizzites, Hivites, and Jebusites. The land was good and large, flowing with milk and honey—and a land with milk and honey will definitely get people's attention. God didn't mention the warfare they would face during this journey, because He wanted to train them and make them strong. God wants His people to be strong and courageous because the kingdom can be obtained only by forceful people.

When we started our ministry in the Bronx, I took spiritual warfare lightly, but I started dreaming about getting shot and being surrounded by armored cars. But when I remembered to put on the whole armor of God and fought a good warfare of faith along with some members, we overcame and the ministry was established. All God's children can be overcomers if only we will be obedient to His call.

In 2 Samuel 5, when David was finally anointed as king over all Israel and Judah, he and his men went to Jerusalem. That land belonged to the Jebusites, who believed that the city and its people were strong enough to prevent King David and his army from coming there. Second Samuel 5:6–7 tells us that David led his troops to Jerusalem to fight against the Jebusites who lived there. "You'll never come in here," they told him. "Even the blind and lame could keep you out," they said, for they thought they were safe. But David and his troops defeated them and captured the stronghold of Zion, now called the city of David. The Jebusites' saying was an insult to this anointed king of God. David knew his strength, he knew his God, and he knew the fortified city would be a good place for a king to build his palace. So he fought and seized it to renovate it to his taste and, according to his power, built a fortified wall around it all and called it the city of David.

That kind of warfare has continued even to this day. When the children of Israel and their neighbors fought to take that land, which they knew that God, the creator of heaven and earth, had given to them, they encountered many difficulties. Some couldn't make it to the land that God had promised to them, a land flowing with milk and honey. But the things they encountered are still with us today, and even more so because, unlike in those days, the enemy battles with our minds. When we walk by sight and operate in the flesh, we lose the war. Neither the Jebusites nor their city's strong walls could stop David from capturing that city for Israel because with his shepherd's strength, nothing was impossible.

Some years ago, when the Lord laid it on my heart to write this book, I responded immediately by getting my pen ready. But the Jebusite in my life prevented me from writing for years, with all kinds of impossibilities and limitations. It wasn't going well. When we disobey God in any area of our lives and put our desires first, He won't give us the wisdom and strength we need to perform the tasks He has called us to do. Church, we are all called to conquer and to rule. If God has given you a vision or desire to do something for Him, don't delay any longer. Don't listen to any negative thoughts with which the enemy will try to limit you. We are called to walk by faith and not by sight. The enemy will try all he can to prevent you from entering your Jerusalem. He knows that when you get there, he will be under your feet and you will rule with the King of Kings. The joy of the earth is at Mount Zion.

Second Corinthians 10:5–6 talks about casting down arguments and every high thing that exalts itself against the knowledge of God, bringing every thought into captivity to the obedience of Christ, and being ready to punish all disobedience when your obedience is fulfilled. The scripture demonstrates that King David cast out all the arguments and the things that he imagined could happen between him and the Jebusites, The high walls around that city could not intimidate David, because he had the knowledge of the living God. So he defeated the Jebusites.

When we receive a scripture, we must respond to it immediately. When we are ready to punish all disobedience, we should search our hearts and take inventory of our lives before we engage in any spiritual warfare. When the children of God sin against Him, they are defeated in battle. So instead of casting blame, let us look within ourselves for what can save us more quickly than engaging in a war that we don't understand. Sometimes, as we walk through life, we search for joy in the wrong places. We just want our share of the inheritance right here in this life, but our father, the creator, knows best. Some of us have our inheritance by grace, but we may end up eating pig food. We waste our precious time worrying about what we don't have and what we are supposed to have. Instead, let's focus on what we do have—the waiting kingdom, the New Jerusalem, the never-ending joy. Jesus Christ is the cause of all true joy because He was moved to conquer for the kingdom. When a man receives the glory of God, he enters a new dimension of revelation because it kills the flesh. When the glory of God and the knowledge of the most high become our only source of living, other things and situations can't control our minds and keep us from reaching our Jerusalem.

"And they said to him thus says Hezekiah, this is a day of trouble and rebuke and blasphemy for the children have come to birth but there is no strength to bring them forth"''" (Isaiah 37:3). Some of us have clearly answered God's call but are still doing nothing. We must remember that the church is supposed to be an army. Each one of us is supposed to be in our various departments for our job description. Ephesians 4:8 says, "When ascended on high, he led captivity captive and give men gifts to men."

If you are reading this book and haven't yet discovered your God-given talent, pray and ask God, who is faithful and just, to reveal it to you.

He wants all His children to be productive in His powerful kingdom, and as you travail and wait on Him through fasting and prayers, He will be with you and strengthen you. We don't do things with our own strength but by the Spirit of God. When we avail ourselves, we become channels. It's not by might or power, but by His Spirit, says the Lord, for with God, all things shall be possible.

When Apostle Paul was in prison, he addressed the church as, "I, Paul, a prisoner of Jesus Christ." He turned his prison cell into an office from which he wrote his epistles. Paul knew he was not guilty, but that he was there to defend the gospel, and he counted it all joy and continued to write his letters. When Anna lost her husband at a young age, as described in Luke 2, she ended up in the temple, praying side by side with Simeon to fulfill the prophecy of the Savior's birth. All these men and women overcame their Jebusites to get to their Jerusalem. Most of the time, we lack knowledge from the Word of God. We are unprepared for the challenges we face as Christians, but the Bible clearly says that our faith will be tested by fire. The enemy is always trying to delay and stop us from reaching our Jerusalem, but we need an overcoming faith to defeat him and move on.

In Genesis, when the blood-soaked cloth of Joseph was shown to Jacob, the evidence was so strong that nothing could console him. But this incident led to his journey to enjoy milk and honey in the midst of a great famine that could have wiped out Jacob and his family. Children of God, your Jebusites are your Jerusalem. Any trial is an opportunity for spiritual growth, our promotion toward our heavenly home. We have so much power in us, but we don't know how to use it. Sometimes the enemy comes and scares us.

One early morning when I was going to a job interview, I didn't have enough time to wait on the Lord. It was a morning rush hour, the weather was cold, and the train was crowded. A schoolboy with his backpack collapsed in the train and fell at my feet. Everyone was trying to do something to help, but I sat there quietly. Like Jonah, I didn't respond because my mind was on the interview. But when I looked at the boy's face, I became frightened. His nose was bleeding badly. I placed my hand on his forehead and prayed a simple silent prayer. Immediately, he was back on his feet. Someone had already called for help, so an ambulance was waiting at the next station. By then, however, the boy looked like nothing had happened to him. Immediately the enemy whispered to me that it wasn't my prayer that healed the boy, because the boy hadn't really been badly injured. But the Holy Spirit put this scripture in my heart from 2 Corinthians 4:7, saying, "But we have this treasure in our earthen vessels that the excellence of the power may be of God and not of us." The Jebusite spirit will always intimidate you and put fear in your heart to stop you from functioning in God's vineyard, but we must be very vigilant—because the best belong to us.

Seven Giants That Want to Intimidate You

The Jebusites are first mentioned in Genesis 10:15–16, and also In Deuteronomy 7:1–2, we read this:

> When the Lord your God brings you into the land which you go to possess, and has cast out many nations before you, the Hittites and the Girgashites and the Amorites and the Cannanites and the Perizzites and the Hivites and the Jebusites, seven nations greater and mightier than you.

God ordered the Israelites to completely destroy the Jebusites, together with the other six mighty nations. But the Jebusites protested against King David's arrival (Joshua 15:63) and Judah failed to expel them from Jerusalem, so they continued to live in the city with the children of Judah. Children of God, we can no longer relate to what God has cast out. God gave the instructions because their backbone was already broken. Sometimes we make compromises and even encourage things that are not supposed to be in our lives because of fear and unbelief. But the task couldn't have been completed without wiping out the Jebusites so that Jerusalem, the city of David, could be built. There are seven giant spirits that we need to conquer in life if we are destined to live in the New Jerusalem.

(1) Canaanites are merchants, financial giants, who humiliate us. God warns the New Testament believers about our finances. Canaanites were controlled by greed. In the area of tithing (Malachi 3:10), we must honor God with our possessions and all the first fruits of our increases (Proverbs 3, 9). We should not allow a get-rich-quick mind-set to rule over us, because that is another form of deception.

(2) Hittites are terror giants who bring fear, confusion, and discouragement. The devil is very busy working with this spirit. In these last days, you can't turn on the television without experiencing fear, confusion, or discouragement. Worry comes from fear, and the only thing that will dissolve fear is knowing God's Word, which is the absolute truth. By faith, we stand tall against any obstacle that will come our way. Without faith, we became useless to our God. Our Savior Jesus Christ has handed us everything we need to conquer through His death on the cross and resurrection (Matthew 28:20).

(3) Hivites claim to offer good life. Many religions and philosophers promote the idea that you can get everything you need if you can believe in yourself. You don't need God. Eat, drink, and be merry, for tomorrow you die. Everyone is going to heaven, no matter what you believe in. Some people even believe they can come back in the form of animal or that they will marry seven virgins. But the Bible is clear Hebrews 9:27. And as it is appointed unto men once to die, but after this the judgement."

As believers, we will all stand before the judgment of our Lord, so let's work out our salvation with trembling and fear.

(4) Perizzites were people who had been separated. They lived in unprotected, unwalled villages. As believers, we must separate ourselves from the world and be reconciled to God through salvation in Jesus Christ. Psalm 18:10 tells us that "The name of the Lord is a strong tower. The righteous run into it and is safe." If we confess to have separated ourselves from the world, let's make sure we are abiding under the Lord's protection. Don't allow Perizzite spirit to separate you from God and His Word, for God knows His children.

(5) Girgashites are people who backslide into worldly and carnal actions. As Hebrews 2:1 tells us, "Therefore we ought to give the more earnest heed to the things which we have heard lest at any time we should let them slip." We should not allow the Girgashite spirit to deceive us into believing that once we are saved, we are forever saved. Some people joke about their salvation, believing they can come and go anytime they want, thinking the door will never shut on them. But remember the ten foolish virgins in Matthew 25. If we don't keep the Word of God in our hearts where it belongs, we let things slip. Our carnal minds always want to go to Satan and the things of this world, which will not profit our souls.

(6) Amorites are arrogant and boastful in their speech. We need to check our hearts and tongue. James 3:2 tells us, "For in many things we offend all if any man offend not in word, the same is perfect man, and able also to bridle the whole body." Arrogance can be defined as having an cattitude of superiority, trying to be what you are not. Ministers, let's take caution that the church has ownership, and we are just the supervisors. Our boastful speeches about what God is doing in our lives and ministries are becoming different from preaching the gospel. The name Jesus Christ must appear frequently in our sermons, if at all. This Amorite spirit is really dealing with us. We exaggerate, which is another way of lying, and our stories are too long. Consider the dangerous times the world is moving in now, and preach salvation because many people in our churches are not saved. Jesus said in Luke 17:10, "Likewise ye, when ye shall have done all those things which are commanded you, Say, we are unprofitable servants; we have done that which was our duty to do." May we surrender to the cross and always be humble, for God resists the proud. We are always called to conquer our fears and take the land, the New Jerusalem.

CHAPTER 4

ALONE WITH GOD

❧

———————————————

Lord, help me understand these
passages I am about to read,
and let them enlighten my spiritual understanding.

Whom have I in heaven but You?
And there is nothing on earth
that I desire besides You.
—Psalm 73:25

When we reach a point in our lives when God is everything, no demons—no matter their ranks—will be able to hurt us. We can share our deepest secrets, have long talks, and laugh. Without intimacy with Him, we will never know that God's love for us is unconditional. Even in our most desperate life situations, He never leaves us. When we are drawn away by our own sinful desires to disobey Him, and then we confess and ask for His help, He always gives us His right hand of fellowship. When the children of Israel were in captivity in Babylon, Ezekiel was with them. We read in Ezekiel 1:1 that the prophet was there to give comfort because they were all in agony. While they were weeping, the heavens opened and he saw the glory of the Lord, greater than the Jerusalem, which can never be taken away or destroyed by any terror attack.

Maybe you're reading this book because you've lost your wealth. Don't worry, because it's about time you opened your spiritual eyes and see the glory of God. You will be refreshed. It happened with the prophet in Isaiah 6, Where it says that when the king Uzziah in our lives dies, our only desire will be the Lord. We have gone through many experiences in life. Most of our songs express the love we have for Him, but they do not follow our lifestyle. I've seen men and women who have been called into the ministry and at the point of their needs they left the ministry to pursue their personal desires. They could not take the pressure from all the singles conferences and had not met anyone to marry them. This is an area where the church needs to take caution. Most ministers take it upon themselves to arrange marriages in their churches to maintain membership. When we come to God with any hidden desire and confess to love Him, He can wash away that desire and prove that He loves us.

I know God called Adam and Eve to live as a couple and have a family, but it didn't turn out that way because of their desires. But God's Word says that when we seek first His kingdom, all other things will be added to us. Sometimes we don't exactly ask for His will. The church is going through the same problem as the worldly people because we all have the same desires. Most of the court television cases are relationship problems. People living as couples and not married always end up fighting in their relationships. Instead of wasting our life with all these desires, why don't we reach out to God to give us our heart's desire? When that becomes our focus, we end up in troubles and sometimes death.

We have not touched the deep wells of God's love. It took me a long time to see that living in that realm can't be compared with anything in this life. There is much joy in the kingdom of God, Everything is passing away except the Word of God. As the world unfolds to its end, must we continue to pursue things that will not bring satisfaction? He is the father to the fatherless and a husband to the widow and a father to all. He works in mysterious ways and works behind the scene toward a perfect conclusion. Amos 5:4–5 says, "For thus says the Lord to the house of Israel: 'Seek me and live; but do not seek Bethel, and do not enter into Gilgal Or cross over to Beer Sheba; for Gilgal shall surely go into exile, and Bethel shall come to nothing.'" We must be obedient to God on this earth because anything else will crush our soul to make us grieve the Holy Spirit. After fasting and praying some of us go back to our sinful desires of thinking, for the joy of all the earth is Mount Zion. It will be a waste of time to go back to Egypt in the wilderness of life when there is nothing left for you to treasure anymore.

When All You Have Is God

Apostle Paul wrote most of his letters from prison, when he was in such a condition that all his soul cried for was his maker, the master. Joseph was taken away from his family and ended up in prison. Even there he was faithful to his God and became a prime minister in Egypt. At that stage in his life, all he wanted was God, so when Potiphar's wife tempted him, he never gave in. If you truly know that you don't have anyone on earth to call upon when you are in trouble or financially broke, you will definitely do the will of God—no matter how lost you are. Daniel discovered this secret.

We Have Nothing But God

We are in this life and in transition to an eternal destination, an everlasting life. For some of us, it looks like we are staying here forever, but we are all going to die one way or the other, since we came from

God, we will return to stand before Him to be judged. This Paul admonished in 1 Timothy 6:5, which says, "For we brought nothing into this world and it is certain, we can carry nothing out." That means that no matter how you try to gain and acquire things, you can't take even a pin with you. That is true. Babies come out of the womb, some with a fixed hand to grab and get hold of things, and yet any dead person has loose, hanging hands. This is the mentality that a carnal mind has, but thanks be to our Lord Jesus Christ, who has saved us and given us His mind-set to be mindful of heavenly things and the things of God. No wonder in some tribes when a king dies, they kill people to allow their spirit to go and serve the dead king. I remember what one of my Bible school teachers said: the road to eternal life is so narrow that you can't take anything with you; it's just you and God. Family and properties are the things God blesses us with to enjoy in this life for a season. We didn't create them. That is why it is certain that we carry nothing out.

Godliness Produces Contentment

Our Lord Jesus Christ, our example, was so content with His father that He was always saying and doing only what He saw or heard His father do. When He was on earth, He had a family, yet He was able to focus and fulfill the will of His father. He knew where He came from and where He was going, so the things of this life could never get ahold of Him, not even death. He pleased the father. In the book of Acts, His disciples followed His examples and did many things in His name to glorify God. The question now for us believers is, are we following Christ's example or we are creating our own righteousness by interpreting scriptures to support whatever we are doing and to claim it as the call of the Holy Spirit? Why are we so different? Are we content with what Christ did for us, or was it not enough for some of us? It took me a long time to learn this truth, and when I found it, I became content because I made God the source of all my joy and Jerusalem above become my chief joy. When the contentment with our God doesn't show in our character or our lifestyle, our children and those around us can't be moved or obey whatever we say or preach to them. Discontentment is a sign that we lack fulfillment. The overflow of the Holy Spirit was necessary for the outpouring on the day of Pentecost.

Apollos was an eloquent man and mighty in scriptures. He was even fervent in his teachings and taught accurately the things of the Lord (Acts 18:24–28). He did all these things only through the baptism of John. He was not filled or baptized in the Holy Spirit, yet he was in his time one of the most powerful evangelists of God's, preaching and drawing crowds by the Grace of God. Aquila and Priscilla were filled and had a gift of discernment. They were able to call Apollos and explain to him the way of God, which is the infilling of the Holy Spirit, and after that, a door was open to him for the brethren to receive him and allow him to do a mighty work of God.

We see more of these Apollonian things in the church. Who are you to contest and give good direction? Apollos was not doing things more accurately. Apollos, with only John's baptism by then could have been a mighty minister without the Holy Spirit, and we will hear that a minister is teaching another gospel or having an affair with one of his members because of the lack of power of the Holy Spirit in his life. Without the infilling, there will be a void in our hearts. You will never be converted, no matter how many souls you win for the kingdom or how many gifts you have and regardless of whether you are called. You will be rejected at the presence of God at the judgment day. Genesis 1:2 tells us that when God created heaven and earth, it was without form and void and darkness was still on the face of the deep, until the Holy Spirit set it in motion. Then God began to speak things into existence, so when we turn to Christ, His Spirit fills us and turns the darkness away. Godliness without contentment also robs us of all the benefits God has granted us. You can be content only when you are filled and led by His Spirit. "For as many as are led by the Spirit of God, these are the sons of God" (Romans 8:14).

God in Man

"And the angel answered and said to her, 'The Holy Spirit will come upon you, and the power of the highest will overshadow you. And that holy one who is to be born will be called the Son of God'" (Luke 1:38).

The Love of God

God's love to mankind is without limit. That's why we should not substitute God's love for anything else. The Holy Spirit came upon a virgin girl called Mary and performed a miracle so that she could give birth. He could have chosen to come in any form, yet He chose a womb to demonstrate how humble He is and that He can live in man. The Holy Spirit in us produces holiness, and that is what He is still doing— living in man in the form of the Holy Spirit to produce righteous fruits. How quickly we forget that God is residing in us in the form of His Spirit. It is this Spirit that will guide us.

God in us is so holy that our physical appearance should reflect His glory anywhere we go. Our houses and our clothes should all be clean. We should be sensitive to the Holy Spirit to the extent that we can't even be by ourselves in our home and allow our clothes and dishes to be dirty and move with impure thoughts and gossip. The thing is, He is checking us all out every second, so don't let the devil deceive you that God is just watching you when you're at the altar and on the church pew to see how best you perform. When we come to the open, we are all alone with Him. From this world till the day of our departure, we will be alone with Him. When all that you have is God, then you have it all because God is all and all is God. We will meet Him in the New Jerusalem, our final destination. When we make plans and leave God out because of our disobedience, we miss it all.

The woman at the well of Samaria in John 4 was fulfilling her life with the flesh, trying to keep a man in her life, thinking that would fill her void. Daughters of Zion, please read carefully the answer that Jesus gave to this woman, and let it be your word. The master did not talk about how to get and keep a man; He went straight to the point. He didn't ask her to put her name in magazines for Christian singles. Natural and physical water needs to be drunk continuously to keep the body going. We need six to eight glasses a day to keep a perfect body. For people without the Spirit of Christ, one woman or one man is not enough. If they can't have it like that, they have to divorce the old spouse and get a new one. Some couples will stay together just for the sake of the ministry and treat each other without love. They stand before God and say, "We have been together in marriage for fifty or sixty years, but out of all those years, just ten of them were truly enjoyable." Tell us what you did with those years and you will receive the applause of men, but God will be the final judge, so be faithful in how you treat your wife or husband so that we will enjoy blessings in our marriage.

Our Lord wants to once and for all quench our thirst in this life by giving Himself in the form of living water. The Bible did not mention the name of the woman because her situation or experience are shared by many women. Some women have lost their salvation and their calling because of these issues. Some have lost their minds and are insane in asylums. A few years ago the Lord led our ministry to raise funds to bless some of these women who through marital issues have lost their minds and are residing in mental institutions. When Jesus asked the woman at the well to call her husband, she was right; she didn't go and call her boyfriend. The Lord saw her honesty. None of her five husbands had stayed with her, so maybe she decided to have them in this friendly way because there is pleasure in secret sins for a season.

Husbands, wives, children, and properties are all added things that God uses to bless mankind. The kingdom is mighty and suffers violence, and you can't be violent when you are always distracted by these additional things. It's wonderful to have family and these things, but if it's not God's time, then we must continue to wait on Him and seek His will concerning these matters. He will surely give us our heart's desire if it's His will and timing. If we truly want Him to choose our inheritance for us, He is our God, and in Him we should trust. God is our heavenly father who also makes sure He fulfills our natural needs that even our earthly fathers can't. Immediately after she perceived that Jesus was not an ordinary man, the woman wanted to know the true worship. Her life was never the same because she had come in contact with Jesus, the source of a fulfilled life. She didn't even go home to her boyfriend but went to the city and everywhere telling people about Jesus. When we are so close to destiny, when all that we have left is God and no more time, get into His business, for something beyond our imagination is waiting for us.

The Lord Is My Shepherd and Your Only One

46

The Lord was David's shepherd because he was a shepherd to sheep and knew how frail these animals are. They depend upon their shepherds for all their needs. They don't know their left from their right. In making God his shepherd, David totally surrendered his entire life to God. When David sinned against God, he totally repented. He didn't want the Lord to desert him by taking his spirit from him. He was a king with multitudes of men and women, children and family members around him, yet he was afraid to be lonely from God. That should be our fear and dread too.

As children of God we shouldn't fear silence. There are people who can't be by themselves for thirty minutes. If they are not waiting on the Lord, they will immediately call a friend or switch on the TV. God can never get their attention. Cell phones have taken over most of our lives. There are people who turn on their cell phones every minute, even in the midst of church sermons. Sometimes when we visit loved ones at the hospital, no matter how much we love them, we must leave them when visiting hours are over. Beloved, we can't always be with people. Let's get used to being alone with God. Sleeping in the same bed with your spouse doesn't mean you go to sleep together and wake up at the same time. You will always be alone, but if you don't know Him, you can't be with Him. People kill themselves because life is unbearable. The unbeliever will do anything to keep himself going with all sorts of addictions, but if you are a believer, this is your joy: a promise of an ever-abiding comforter the Holy Spirit will forever be with you (John 14:16). You will never be alone. You'll always be with God, from everlasting to everlasting.

CHAPTER 5

PRAY TO SEE HIS GLORY

❦

The New Jerusalem is all about God's glory. What is the definition of *glory*? According to the dictionary it means praise, honor or distinction extended by a common consent, renowned wonderful praise and thanksgiving. Something that secures praise, a highly recommendable asset.

Magnificence, something marked by beauty slender, beatific happiness of heaven.

A height of prosperity or achievement to rejoice proudly.

Yes all these descriptions fitted our God's glory and even more than what an eye could describe.

And he said, "Show me, I pray thee, thy glory" (Exodus 33:18). God exactly knew what Moses was asking: to see His face, to see what God looks like. Moses saw a burning bush and heard a voice and kept on hearing the voice, but that wasn't enough for him. Man always wants to see, feel, and touch, but God is a Spirit. "And He said, Thou cannot see my face; for man shall not see Me and live" (Exodus 33:20).

Moses went to the mountain, but in all the forty days he spent with God, he never saw God's physical face, but the back of God, and even passing by, you need to hide in the crack of a rock. Yet the children of Israel could not behold the face of Moses unless through a veil. The will of God for us was expressed when Jesus declared that "He who has seen Me has seen God" (John 14:8–9). Philip was kind of skeptical because maybe he realized that no one can see the father and live and that even Moses, who saw the father's back, had to put a veil on for the Israelites to come near him and talk to him. In Revelation, John saw the real glory when he saw Jesus. "And when I saw Him, I fell at His feet as one dead and He laid His right hand upon me, saying, 'Fear not: I am the first and the last'" (Revelation 1:17). John fainted and passed out while he was very in the spirit. If he had been in the flesh, he would have been passed out at a glance. That's why God admonishes us to worship Him in the spirit because flesh and blood can never inherit the kingdom of God.

Prayer reveals God's glory in Luke 9:28–36 in an incident called the transfiguration, when Jesus took Peter, John, and James and went up to a mountain to pray. In the course of the prayer, the Bible says, the fashion of his countenance was altered, his garment became white and shining, and Moses and Elijah came and talked with him. Peter encouraged the Lord to make tabernacles for Moses and Elijah, and one for the master himself. But Peter was not ready for one, nor was John or James. He just wanted to jump ahead of the cart, not knowing what he was suggesting. While talking to Jesus, God spoke through a cloud. I believe the sight would have been fearful. God confirmed with His own voice that Jesus Christ was His beloved son, so all should hear Him: Jesus Christ, our great and only Savior, took time out of His busy life to pray and still spent time with the father. This should be our pattern too. He went to the mountain to pray. His father was so happy with Him in front of those disciples for them to know that they were not just following any man but the Son of God, who is also the glory of the father.

Beloved, we should pray and see truly who Jesus is, to see His glory that will reflect in our lives and ministries because we are serving a glorious God. Jesus asked His disciples, in John 6:67, when people were leaving His ministry because they couldn't take the truth of His teaching, whether they would also go. Peter, one of the disciples who were with Jesus at the transfiguration, was quick to answer that there is no life without Jesus. He is the one who has the Word of eternal life because no one in his or her right mind will see such a glory and turn his back and walk away to damnation. Beloved, if we have tested and seen the Savior Jesus Christ, let us walk away from all our fleshly desires as the world is heading toward gross darkness. Let us proclaim the gospel without fear because we are commissioned to do so. The apostle Peter did really love the Lord. In the garden of Gethsemane (John 18:10) he demonstrated his love by cutting the ear of Malchus, the servant of the high priest. He also promised to die with the Lord. I believe this means that even after he denied Jesus, the Lord knew Peter loved Him, and so the Lord corrected him. If you truly see and taste the glimpse of the Lord's glory, you will forever love Him regardless of what you go through in the service of His kingdom.

In Luke 2:25–39, Simeon and Anna prayed to see God's glory. By revelation Simeon was always in the temple with Anna, praying and fasting night and day for the fulfillment of the messianic prophecy of Jesus Christ. Because you have to want it, to receive it, Simeon was waiting for the consolation of the promise because the Holy Ghost was upon him. In these end times what are we praying about? We need to focus on the same pattern for Christ's second coming, that the church will wake up from its sleep and evangelize by prayer and fasting to prepare Christ's bride for Him to come in His glory. Simon saw the glory of Jesus Christ before His departure from this life to eternity.

What a reflection for people to know and accept Jesus Christ and see His glory before that doomsday when it will be too late for many people. Anna, a prophetess who lost her husband after just seven years of marriage, decided to use the rest of her life in the house of the Lord to see this glory. How many men and women can pay this price in our day to see a glimpse of this glory, when most of us are full of ourselves and just what we and our family need? It's just me and my ministry and everyone else can perish. May God deliver us from self-wants and focus on what the world needs now: Jesus Christ.

Jacob also prayed and saw God's glory. In Genesis30:32 And Jacob called the name of the place Penile: For I have seen God face to face and my life is preserved. Jacob at that point in his life went into prayer before God to see His glory and for his life to be preserved because he has had a dream about it. God revealed His glory by touching the hollow of Jacob's thigh, and by this glory was the name and the nation of Israel revealed. When we spend time in prayer, God will definitely reveal His glory to direct our path into light. Jacob had waited on the Lord at Manama, which has a biblical meaning of two camps, by leaving his family at one camp and keeping another one with the Lord. We always need two camps, and the one with our Lord is very important, and the one with our fellowship with others. If you really want to see his glory, there are things He will reveal to you when you are alone with Him. If Jacob had met Esau without the presence of the Lord, the cause of his destiny would have changed, but thank God for His unfailing promises that the seed of Abraham will save the earth. Once we come in contact with God's glory, we can never go back to anything that does not glorify God, because it is from glory to glory. He reveals his truth to us because our praise is secured. It is also a highly recommended asset that has economic value and ownership of God's kingdom.

God's glory will transform us totally, and everything else in this life will be meaningless when you see His glory. After seeing God's glory, Jacob was able to face Esau without fear, even when Esau was still suggesting they go to Seir together and live. Jacob refused. When you see God's glory, you cannot compromise with anything that will diminish the glory upon your life. Our yes will be yes and our no will be no.

Peter also prayed and saw God's glory: "And saw heaven opened, and a certain vessel descending upon him, as it had been a great sheet knit at the four corners, and let down to the earth" (Acts 10:11). Peter went up upon the house to pray and fell into a trance and saw heaven open. Prayer and fasting will always reveal God's glory. We didn't know what Peter was praying about, but based on what they were going through at the time, it may have been something that concerned the kingdom and lost souls. How can such a God who created the whole world send His only begotten son to die for just one nation? Most at the time did not believe even in His son. It was through this trance that God revealed to Peter that the Gentiles could also receive the Holy Ghost. Some are clean, so Peter should not call them commoners.

The glory that unfolds to us through prayer and fasting is awesome, with great revelation. In this great revelation Peter revealed that God was unfolding this glory, that the Gentiles also could become heirs by faith through the Abrahamic covenant. In Numbers 14:11–22 after the children of Israel disobeyed and doubted God, Moses interceded, but God made a profound declaration that His glory would not be seen by them alone but that the whole earth will be filled with His glory. He did this by sending His only begotten son to die for the whole world.

No matter where you come from, if you serve Jesus as the Lord your Savior, God's glory will be revealed to you and direct your steps to the heavenly Jerusalem. As believers preparing to meet His final glory, our behavior and attitude should reflect His magnificent, splendid, and beautiful happiness that will encourage souls to crave for His lordship. A height of prosperity is from His blessings, not achieved through dubious ways such as twisting scriptures to gain for our own selfish desires. A good name is always better than riches, which come from God and achievements. We rejoice proudly that we can say with Apostle Paul, "I have fought a good fight. I have finished the race; I have kept the faith so we will be ready" (2 Timothy 4:7).

The Lord will grant us the crown of righteousness and glory. All the conflict we are engaging in every day will not be a problem at all because through it, His glory will be revealed. Seeking our own glory will not go well for us. It will mean that another gospel is preached it will be a blasphemy, it won't go well with us because we don't want to get into his presence only to be rejected because the things we did in his name did not reflect his glory. For we cannot bypass the cross and seek His glory; our flesh must be crucified. There are things in our lives that will hinder us. There are little foxes that we neglect but that destroy the vine. A lady in our fellowship saw a vision of Christ directing people in a crossway. Some were pointed to the left and others to the right. She was directed to the right way. As she was going, she discovered a sign engraved with the word *Love*. There were not many people on that way, but when she saw the *Love* sign she knew she was on her right way home to be with the Lord.

Lack of love within the church will cause us shipwreck. If we truly have His spirit of love, it will not be a problem at all because the Lord always reveals His glory through love. At the appointed time God revealed His glory through his son Jesus Christ to save mankind. What a privilege for us to have such a Savior to be born and walk on this earth. Our once-born king was not a prince, because only a prince can inherit a throne. That is why Herod was terrified. He had never heard such a thing as a born child being a king while all those earthly kings inherited their father's throne because they were born into the royal families and therefore had the chance to become king. People in other religions can't take it that Jesus is God, but prophecy was given before His birth.

"For unto us a child is born, unto us a son is given; and his government shall be upon his shoulders, and his name shall be called wonderful counselor, mighty God, everlasting father, prince of peace" (Isaiah 9:6). Please pay attention to the titles each one carry a weight of glory that will blow your carnal mind if you did not believe it. God entered his son to redeem the world back with him because an everlasting father will always have everlasting kingdom and everlasting children. Let's pray to see his glory, it will transform us.

CHAPTER 6

ARE YOU WEARY IN WAITING?

❧

But they that wait upon the Lord
shall renew their strength;
They shall mount up with wings as eagles,
they shall run and not be weary.
—Isaiah 40:31

Waiting? How long? In this fast-paced world of the Internet and fast food, no one is prepared to wait for anything. But the scripture is admonishing those who serve God and are waiting for the second coming of Christ to wait upon the Lord. This kind of waiting is not a standstill or a sit and wait. Scripture reading and meditation also transform our mind. It gives us hope and joy of God's promises, a kingdom mind-set, to read Luke 1 about Elizabeth and Zechariah. The Bible says they were both righteous before God, walking in all the commandments of God, yet Elizabeth was barren. But Zechariah was performing his pastoral duties. He trusted his God, he waited on Him as a minister, and he also studied the Word. He knew that with God, all things are possible. He recalled what God did for Sarah and Abraham. His faith was not shaken.

These days we would rather find a quick way to fulfill our own desires. No one wants to wait on God. We've been seeing and hearing how men and women "of God" are buying powers to grow their ministries at all costs. How pitiful instead of waiting on the Holy Spirit for directions we go by our flesh to gain popularity with all these numerous membership which does not please God. Child of God, the church is the Lord's and we are called to serve as we continue to wait on the Lord. He will renew our old ways and strengthen us to wait on Him. If Zechariah were living in our times, he would receive prophesies about why the wife is not giving birth. A man like him should have children to take over the ministry when he is old, yet the Bible was specific about both of them that although they were holy and righteous, they never knew Elizabeth's womb was reserved for the baptizer of Jesus. The timing was all from God and not witchcraft. Zechariah was running in and out of the church but was not weary. He loved the Lord, who had called him to serve.

This story was told by one of my senior pastors about a missionary who was sent to a remote part of the world for mission work. For the first seven years not one person from the village joined the church despite all the evangelistic work he did. He became weary and asked his head office to recall him home and send someone else. That week a miracle happened. The village chief's wife was bleeding to death on the labor bed. She asked for a prayer from the pastor, and someone quickly ran for him. As soon as he prayed, the blood ceased and the baby was born safely. The following week the church was filled. He called and canceled his transfer. All the true waiting for the seven years had been fulfilled, so why are we deceiving ourselves that the gift of God can be bought with money? As Peter told Simon in Acts 8, the Holy Spirit can't be bought with money. Rather, anyone who tries to buy it will perish with his money as Judas Iscariot perished with his money.

When we accept the Lord as our Savior, we enter into a kingdom that is governed by a king with diversities of administrative and operational gifts. No unbelievers will understand this kingdom message, that the governance of Christ's kingdom is faith and works. That's why every child of God is giving gifts and talent to keep us doing this kingdom work to show forth God's glory.

Waiting upon this gracious God is not weariness but a joy. A good waiter always gets a good tip because he always focuses on his assigned task to make sure all the customers' needs are quickly met. Some will just prioritize your water or coffee as soon as they see the need to. Our waiting on the Lord is making sure that each and every person is busy working in the kingdom using the gift and talent the Lord has given him. In Psalm 28:7 and in Nehemiah 8:10, the prophet encourages people of Israel after a long silence of not hearing from God because of their captivity and their temple's destruction. They were encouraged to go home and rejoice, not to be sorrowful, for the joy of the Lord was their strength. Any child of God who is always sorrowful and sad should quickly go back to reread the Bible. Knowing that somebody loves and cares for you will always give you strength to carry on no matter what. For God so loved the world that He gave a gift of joy: Jesus Christ. I don't see why, if you have truly received Him into your heart, you still walk around with a heavy heart filled with mourning and complaining, with no desire to do anything for the Lord because you have no energy. The energy you have is just for yourself but not for things of God. Many Christians are constantly depressed, with no energy even to read the Bible or pray.

The Eagle's Wings

An eagle is a large, powerfully built bird with a heavy head and beak. It has relatively longer and broader wings and a faster, more direct flights. Most very large eagles have powerful eyes, which enable them to spot potential prey from a long distance. Eagles are such powerful birds that in ancient times, people worshipped them as gods. They are also seen in the coat of arms of many nations. The symbol of the eagle is recognized. No wonder the almighty God, the creator of the universe, who created the bird, chose the imagery of an eagle to describe His love for His people. Their wings are so very long and large that it takes a lot of energy to flap them. Their wings are wide enough to carry their own body weight plus things they catch. That's why scientists have discovered eagles can fly very long distances especially during migration. They often soar on thermals until they reach a great altitude. They also use the gliding method of flying to cover the longest distance using small amounts of energy.

God almighty is encouraging His people to just wait upon Him. In doing so, we will acquire such strength and energy to move ahead in our Christian walk, whether in the ministry or family matters. What an awesome God we have, that we can soar or migrate to His presence in heaven, which lies far above all principalities and powers taking dominion over spiritual wickedness in high places. But sometimes when we break our fellowship, we walk around with chicken wings and have no energy to fly. We wait on Him by reading our Bibles every day, evangelizing, praying, and giving in faith. You cannot go wrong on these lines.

Beloved, let's do His work in love. Christianity is not a religion. It is not a performance and acceptance. It is a relationship we can't be weary of when we are encouraging others for their need for a Savior, Jesus Christ, and recognizing their need of repenting from their sins. "For all have sinned and fall short of the glory of God" (Romans 3:23). We believe in Jesus and His power to save them, "for God so loved the world that He gave His only begotten son, that whoever believes in Him should not perish, but have eternal" (John 3:16). They need to receive His salvation for Him to live in their hearts. His promise is very clear. "But as many as received Him, He gave them the right to become the children of God" (John 1:12). They have to confess their faith, the Bible assures us: "If we confess with our mouth that Jesus is Lord, and believe in our hearts that God raised Him from the dead, you will be saved" (Romans 10:9). But we also, testifying about our lives, and what the Lord has done for us, will be a great encouragement. If we are doing this kingdom work, I don't see how we can become wearied.

The Holy Spirit was poured on the disciples for an empowerment for ministry. "But you will receive power, when the Holy Spirit comes upon you and you shall be my witnesses for both in Jerusalem Judea and Samaria unto the utmost part of the earth" (Acts 1:8). That was the first outpouring, so when we receive Jesus, we're baptized in the Spirit and empowered to continue in the same services unto the Lord. We have exchanged the heavy yokes around our necks for Christ's light yoke so that we can soar and do this kingdom work without feeling any burden or weariness. On the day you feel like giving up, murmuring and complaining, remember the big picture that shows not only that you are helping to build a legacy….. for your family but that your tireless efforts have eternal value as long as we have the Holy Spirit. We can do all things for and through Christ, who gives us everything we need to serve Him.

Physical waiting is difficult and wearisome, especially when you don't know when the next bus or train will be arriving. Some people would rather walk and get more tired than wait. In Exodus 32:1–35, when the people of Israel saw that Moses was not coming when they expected, they quickly got busy by sinning against God. They made themselves a handmade god they could see like that of other nations because most of them had lived in Egypt all their lives, so idol worshipping was not a new thing to them. They couldn't have faith in God, who delivered them from the hands of Pharaoh for four hundred years, and couldn't wait for Moses for forty days. I wonder, as I read the passage from the Bible, where were they in a hurry to get to? So it is in our days: children of God cannot wait on God for directions. Their behavior causes many to fall into Satan ditches. Some people get busy during their waiting period to fill their void. Even so, the woman in Proverbs 7:18–20 engaged in prostitution because her husband was traveling on a long journey. He would not be back soon; he went with a lot of money. She even knew the time of his arrival and couldn't wait that long. She needed to fill the lust in her heart with another man. But we don't know the time of our Lord's coming and can't engage in any earthly desire that doesn't profit us and the kingdom.

Dear beloved child of God, we will never be weary because our God never gets weary. He is the owner of the universe, and without Him there will be no creation. We have known and heard that He is an everlasting God. He can't faint or get weary. So like a father with his children, we carry His strength and power. (He has given us the authority.) In fact, any time we wait on Him, He increases our strength to our years. The young with strength and vigor can faint and lose power, but we who have accepted His only begotten son with His abiding Spirit will never faint or grow weary. We can walk and run miles for the kingdom and will not get weary, because it's not by might or power but the infilling of the Holy Spirit. We will soar like the eagle and meet Him in the air. Oh, what a day it will be to meet Jesus face-to-face. Let's continue to wait on Him, for sooner or later it will surely happen.

The spirit of restlessness
This is a spirit that will

Wrestle with believers

- Saul couldn't wait for Samuel as he instructed him earlier (1 Samuel 13:13), and the consequences cost him his kingdom and his title as king.
- Abraham couldn't wait for God's promise, and we are all suffering and paying the price for it (Genesis 16).
- Samson went to a gala and saw a prostitute. He couldn't wait to find out who she was. He didn't have time to propose and marry her (Judges 13).
- Adonijah, one of David's sons, couldn't even wait till his father's death. He wanted to become a king by appointing himself. It didn't go well with him (1 Kings 1).

Many believers can't wait on God until they fulfill their vows at the altar. They just give in and sleep with their partners. We see the results in many marriages—divorce. They just simply can't wait; they are too much in "love." By doing this, you give a foothold to the devil in marriage. If you've already done that, pray and ask God for forgiveness. Parents should teach their children very well.

It all started in the garden of Eden when the devil talked to the woman. She couldn't wait for his next visit to inquire from her husband. If it was true, she could still eat the fruit. That's where the spirit of disobedience and restlessness began. Men and women of God who travel and leave their partners behind give up sometimes and break the marriage because they can't wait any longer. Well, if we are not waiting on God, where are we going to get our strength from? I remember a story that a pastor told me about attending a conference in a nearby state. After he returned from the conference to his hotel, he discovered that a bottle of champagne was waiting for him in an ice bucket with a lot of treats. He claimed that was part of the package. Within a few minutes this gorgeous lady knocked on his door and asked if the pastor needed company and suggested that they enjoy the champagne together. He was wearing his wedding ring. The pastor told her to remove the ice bucket and go and repent. He was a pastor and a married man with children, and the hotel was hosting a pastors' conference. They were there to wait on the Lord, not themselves. Church, we need to wait on the Lord at all times. The spirit of the antichrist is everywhere to defy us and is looking to destroy Christ bride if possible. We should be vigilant and raise our spiritual antennas everywhere we go.

Jacob was able to wait for seven years to marry Rachel (Genesis 29). Jacob, the foundation of the nation of Israel, was tested and tried by true love. It is the genealogy of David and our Savior, Jesus Christ. God chose Israel for a good reason. He needed a nation to be called His own, that has a strong foundation of true love. Rachel who gave birth to Joseph, the preserver of Israel. He quickly forgave his brothers and helped them survive through the famine. Because Jacob was able to wait 7 years and marry Rachel, and gave birth to Joseph to help build the nation of Israel. I don't think many men these days could do that waiting. Jacob is not all that bad as we read about him with his deceptive tricks. God has been good to us for not killing us while we were living in sin. He patiently waited to save us. We should always wait on Him for our final instructions as we prepare to meet Him sooner or later.

CHAPTER 7

HEPHZIBAH: A NEW NAME FOR ZION

---※---

You shall no longer be termed forsaken nor
shall your land any more be termed desolate;
you shall be called Hephzibah and your land Beulah
for the Lord delights in you and
your land shall be married.
—Isaiah 62:4

This is a passage in the Bible that gives believers every encouragement they need to understand that rejection and isolation will never be their portion in this life. As long as you love the Lord Jesus Christ and are willing to serve Him, you have a new name, Hephzibah, for the Lord surely delights in you. Sometimes we get worried about the gossip around us and our ministries to the extent that we get discouraged and grieve the Holy Spirit by responding negatively, trying to defend ourselves, talking about the situation, and trying to win the sympathy of people who even in their hearts don't love us or care about what we're going through. But the Savior, who knew you before you entered your mother's womb to be born, has found you faithful already and called you to be His minister, and has given you a new name. That name is already written in the Lamb's book of life. The Lord your God, your bridegroom, died and shed His precious blood to redeem you, to change your destiny to live with you in the New Jerusalem. If you really know who you are, then let those who forsake you be in confusion by not paying them any attention, but by focusing on serving the master. Desolation with man versus communion with God: the face of every child of God will go through a period of being forsaken, no matter how wonderful you think you are, or anointed. Let us understand the warfare that accompanies our salvation because the enemy wants us to feel forsaken and desolate and somehow suffer rejection by people we love and call companions.

King David, a man of God's own heart, went through terrible situations; he was forsaken even though he was the Lord's beloved. He expressed it most times in the psalms. King Saul, whom he admired and looked to as a father, was trying to kill him. He was despised for worshipping the Lord, and his own son wanted his throne. Sometimes these insecurities and rejections can lead us astray to the point where a king like David will take someone's wife and have her husband killed. Sometimes when we feel forsaken, our flesh takes over but to be spiritually minded is the increase of peace. When the spirit of rejection comes over people, they sometimes do terrible things. They later kill themselves or kill the one who rejected them, but as children of God we have a father who comforts and strengthens us in our inner man no matter what we face.

Isaiah 54 was a demonstration of God's mercies to the Israelites after He rejected and forsook them, and yet He assured them of their heritage. He began encouraging the barren to break forth into singing and cry aloud. He went on and encouraged the barren to enlarge the place of their tent because faith will always conquer. Our faith in Him always gives us the victory to overcome every unbearable situation we face. In Genesis 17:19, God called Abraham and said, "Sarah your wife shall bear you a son and you shall call him Isaac. I will establish my covenant with him for an everlasting covenant and with his descendants after him and make him fruitful and will multiply him exceedingly he shall beget 12 princes and I will make him a great nation."

God did visit Sarah as He had promised. She had been barren all her life, but at the age of ninety she gave birth to Isaac, the son of promise with whom God established His everlasting covenant, which will lead to the Jerusalem above. Even when Abraham was called to enlarge his field, he stumbled, yet he believed that nothing about God was ever barren or wasted. As you're reading this book, if you feel forsaken or depressed because of any lack in your life, be sure that all things will always work for you as a child of God. We need to get to a new level of spiritual anointing to overcome our obstacles and earthly passions. The promise in Revelation 2:17 says, "He will give a new name written on a stone which no one knows except him who receives it." The status in life that society and tradition has given you is not your real name. It is not even the real name they call us in this life. We have all received one name as of one father. Children in the New Jerusalem are not going to fill out any application for a job or hospital information sheet where they have to declare their status as either male or female, plus their age, color, or race. They'll have just one new name for Zion: Hephzibah. That is our new name. Revelation 3:12 says, "He who overcomes, I will make him a pillar in a temple of my God and he shall go out no more. I will write on him the name of my God and the name of the city of my God. The New Jerusalem which comes from out of heaven from my God and I will write on him my new name."

The Word says he who overcomes will be a pillar in the temple of God. According to 2 Chronicles 3:17 when Solomon built the temple, he set up two pillars before the temple. The right-hand pillar was named Jachin and the left-hand pillar Boaz, meaning the church of God was established in strength, and our strength comes from our

God. As children of God we are stronger than anything the enemy wants to put in our way. If the Lord is our strength, of whom and of what should we be afraid? We are His pillars on earth that support the church. That is why no gates of hell can prevail. That means the gates will try, but we should not allow it, because they are not supposed to prevail against it. We should at all costs support and finance the gospel to reach into all the world as the Word commands us. As pillars we are forever established. The enemy cannot toss us here and there, our faith is grounded already, and we are marked by names only God knows.

A New Name

When Jesus saw Nathanael under the fig tree in John 1:47, He saw a new name written over him that Nathaniel didn't know: behold an Israelite indeed, in whom is no guile. Once a friend told me a story about two people who went to an all-night prayer meeting. On their way home they met a demon-possessed man who quickly named them individually by calling one an Israelite and the other one Egyptian. That is how he saw them spiritually. It is the same with us Christians. Let's face this fact: either we are all for Christ and His kingdom or none of us at all are, for God knows those who are His by identifying them with a new name—the name of the city where we will spend eternity and enjoy an everlasting life. God didn't create us just to live and die and go to heaven. He wants us to begin the excitement of our new home right in this life, with all our possessions.

What Is Naming?

Naming is used to identify and clarify things. After creation, God gave Adam and Eve authority to name things. Do not allow your circumstances to name you. Don't allow any sickness to name you. If you are burdened or in any challenging situation, call the elders of the church because you don't want anything to come between you and your new home above. We should still honor the men and women of God in charge of us because God wants order in the church. God has anointed men and women here with various gifts to edify the church. If you are having a secret passion or problem, don't hesitate. Always call for help and for proper counseling, for we are not dealing with flesh and blood. Words such as *homosexual, pornography,* and *adultery* shouldn't even be mentioned among the body of Christ, for God has called His church with a new name. Don't allow Satan and your circumstance to name you. Sometimes people call us names we are not aware of to identify a certain character we are promoting, so please, stop responding to the women in your church, for they call you a woman's man. Sometimes, too, if the name does not fit you, God will defend you and shame all your gossipers.

Naming is very important to God. In Genesis 17, God changed Abram to Abraham: "Neither shall thy name anymore be called Abram, but Abraham, for a father of many nations" (Genesis 17:5). Abram was the name Abram's father gave him at birth, and it means "exalted father." God called him and fulfilled Abram's name and called him Abraham, father of multitudes. He originally had a good name and I believe it's all the doing of the Lord, but "exalted father" had to become a father to many nations. Our God also is exalted. The whole world belongs to Him. Some of us have names we don't even understand. No wonder in 1 Chronicles 4:10 Jabez cried out to God for a name change. These days people are changing their names to fit biblical phrases such as "blessing," "no weapon," and so forth, but don't worry about your name. God has already named you in Revelation 2:17. As you keep on operating in your overcoming faith, the Lord keeps on feeding you with a hidden manna, and has cut you a white stone and designed a new name on it that no one knows except you. So, dear believer, take the time to endure whatever you need to go through as a good soldier of Jesus Christ, for you will definitely enter the New Jerusalem with a new name.

Joseph in Genesis 41 was a slave in a dungeon, interpreting dreams by using a gift God gave him. He changed his position and his name in Egypt. The chief butler didn't remember Joseph after he got his job back, but we are supposed to give thanks in all things. As one sister said, if the butler had mentioned Joseph to Pharaoh, it may have been that Joseph would have taken the baker's position because it was vacant when he was killed. But after two years, God, who works behind the scenes, came with another plan of dream interpretation that promoted Joseph so that he became a ruler in Egypt. Child of God, stop worrying and stay focused, for the Lord delights in you to give you the kingdom. We weary the Lord with unnecessary demands that will not do us any good in this life. He is also preparing to give you a new name and a new position in the New Jerusalem because the Lord delights in you. He has married you to give you His name, a sign that you belong to Him, and He will not share you with anyone. He is jealous over you to protect you and bring you to His holy hill. "I am my beloved's and his desire is towards me" (Song of Solomon 7:10).

If a man marries a woman, they become one flesh and keep one name—the man's because he initiated the marriage and proposed to the woman. The church of Jesus Christ is His beloved. He proved His love by dying on the cross, and His desire is seriously on His people to bring us to His kingdom and enjoy us forever. Hephzibah will be our new name.

In Genesis 32:24–32 Jacob was Jacob when he deceived his father and took his brother Esau's blessing. He was still Jacob when he ran and lived with his uncle Laban. He wanted to go back, despite the big family and great wealth that accompanied him. He wrestled with the angel of God to bless him. They wrestled all night. It wasn't as easy as when he deceived and took his brother's blessing, so when the angel asked him his name, he responded, "Jacob," and the angel said, "Your name is changed. Your new name is Israel, Child of God." The Lord Jesus Christ has called us into His eternal kingdom. He has given us names that befit our callings—pastors, evangelists, apostles, prophets, teachers, bishops, deacons, elders, and ushers—to work in His vineyard, but of late these names are losing their value. It shouldn't be so. Some of us wrestled in life for God to ordain us with these titles. Let us live up to them. When Jacob became Israel, he was able to face Esau. The favor of God was upon him, and he became a nation.

Chapter 8

Singing the Lord's Song in a Strange Land

❧

How shall we sing the Lord's song in a strange land?

—Psalm 137:4

When the children of Israel were in captivity in Babylon, their captors were making a mockery of them by asking them to sing to them some of their Zion songs. They were right to respond that they couldn't do that, it was impossible because that time it would not be for the glory of the Lord, but for themselves and their captors. In this grace period many Christians do things that are spiritually out of order and approve them with the name of the Lord. But a day is coming when all these works will pass through the fire of assessment and the evidence will be clear. At least they remembered the good that the Lord had done for them in Zion and wept over their situation, a form of repentance. They were trying to be holy by telling their captors such songs couldn't be sung just anywhere. Thank God that through Jesus Christ now we carry God's presence everywhere we go, and we can sing and worship God anywhere. They even swore an oath never to forget Jerusalem again.

Many people sing the Lord's song without having any relationship with Him, especially in the music ministry. God has given us a great talent. They are the Levites who bring heaven down as our praises go up before every service of God begins. Some of them need prayers and support. Their role in the kingdom is vital. The devil is jealous of them because he became arrogant and lost his position in heaven. If every praise and worship leader and all gospel music artists will know that their role in the kingdom is the heartbeat of the church, we will see great transformation in the body of Christ. We can't sing and preach just because we have melodious voices. The Lord is holy and must be served with fear.

Read the description of Lucifer in Isaiah 14:12. Yet he was cast down because of pride. The church declares that we've been saved by grace, yes, and the merciful God hasn't ceased to love us. We can always come to Him and say sorry and He will quickly forgive us if only we are ready to turn away from our sins. Let God applaud us rather than men. Sometimes God is not with the majority. Lucifer became proud because when he sang and all heavenly hosts bowed to the Lord, he mistakenly thought it was for him. Some of the angels believed him to the extent that they followed him to war, and they were all cast down by the Lord. However, without him heavenly worship still continues 24/7. Malachi 1:6 says, "A son honors his father, and a servant his master, if then I am the father, where is my reverence says the lord of hosts. It is you priests who have shown contempt for my name but you ask how we have shown contempt for your name."

Throughout the Bible God has demonstrated His fatherly love and His masterly discipline. First He created this world with love, and when man fell in the garden of Eden, He quickly laid up an everlasting plan of salvation by sending His only begotten son to die and save us. When we study His redemptive plan for salvation, we realize how deep His love is for His creation, creating man in His own image with respect and dignity. When He drove man from the garden of Eden, man came in contact with sin and diseases because what He created was not subject to the kind of atmosphere that man was to live in. Even then He continued to sustain man physically through wisdom and knowledge. He has given to the medical field specializations in each part of the body—the head (all parts) and all the other parts of the body. He also introduced equipment such as X-rays and surgical tools, and medications so that man could still live comfortably on this earth, whether he knew Him or not. He still sends rain and sunshine to the earth, and gives it heat and cold. He also blesses the land with rain for the earth to bring food and drink to man and even to the beasts of the field, and throughout the Bible He has demonstrated His goodness throughout all generations.

All He demands is our honor, so anytime we disobey and break any of His commandments, even if it's through dealing with one another, we are dishonoring Him. Anytime we enter His presence, whether by ourselves or in the assembly of the congregation, He would rather we reconcile and make peace with one another instead of sitting and pretending everything is all right. He always prefers our obedience to our sacrifice. That is why our works are going to go through the fire—the works and the sacrifice we did toward His name while we were living in disobedience, with sins of anger, pride, jealousy, and hatred. We need to remind ourselves that we are not getting away with anything. No matter how beautifully we operate outside ourselves, and no matter how many times we are called to sing or to preach, God is still the same. He doesn't compromise His holiness through the Bible and does not allow His people to get away with sin. Numbers 21:6 says, "So the Lord sent fiery serpents among the people and they bit the people and many of the people of Israel died." God uses many ways to discipline His people, he sent a fiery serpent to bite the Israelites and also used a serpent on a pole to heal and set His people free. Please let's pray for the fear of God to be part of our lives. No wonder David said it is a fearful thing to fall into His hands because there will be no deliverance, and no deliverer means eternal death to the body, soul and spirit, so let us also remember the fury of the Lord. We should not take the grace of God for granted, because we can't sing the Lord's song in a strange land. The enemy mocks us because he knows that our prayers are not affecting anything and God will not accept such worship.

Joshua 24:15 says, "And if it seems evil to you to serve the Lord choose for yourself this day whom you will serve, whether the gods which your fathers served that were on the other side of the river, or the gods of the Amorites, in whose land you dwell, but as for me and my house we will serve the Lord." Being a child of God means being a chosen one, ordained by God to be His child so that we will abide only in Him and He in us. God will spite us for being lukewarm, so anytime we disobey Him, we have voluntarily made a choice to serve whatever we want.

The book of Malachi, the last book of the Old Testament, clearly deals with the sin of the believer. It is the last book to prepare the heart of the believer for the New Testament. It deals with believers who dabble in these kinds of sins, hatred, divorce, ministers who prefer others over their spouses, and robbing God of our tithes and offerings. Joshua was so zealous for the promised land that when he saw the hypocrisy of his people, he declared that it would be better to serve God only or not to serve Him at all, but as for him and his house, he said, they would serve Jehovah. No matter how good or bad the situation looked, he would set his heart on the Lord to get to the Promised Land.

We face the same temptation today. Pornography is an epidemic anywhere we turn, but a mind of Christ and a heart set on a pilgrimage will not move by sight. Sometimes Christians organize parties and family get-togethers and partake in dancing to worldly music, and even serve alcoholic beverages. The Bible says the angels of the Lord encamp around those that fear Him, so when we get into these activities, where do we leave the angels? Do we get them involved in such activities? The eye of the Lord is upon the righteous, so when a believer chooses to commit sin, he is trying to tell God and the guardian angels to leave him for a while. He or she is not ready for the Lord's coming; he would prefer the things of this life to the New Jerusalem.

It's about time we choose whom we will serve instead of wasting the Lord's precious time. The children of Israel rejected God and went into captivity and wept for deliverance. When they repented, the Lord answered them in Psalm 137:1, which says, "By the rivers of Babylon there we sat down yea, we wept when we remembered Zion." They remembered Zion and wept while in captivity, but would not listen and pay heed to the Word of God while they were in Zion as God's children. We are not getting away with unrepented sin and secret sinful pleasures. We will not be tolerated by our God, because where we are going, we can't take anything with us, not even the body we now live in. It's going to be just us and our God. Did we come to this life with clothes from our mother's womb? We always forget that we will leave as we came. We work and toil from morning to night just to make money and gain property, and we don't even know how we will exit this life. But when we die, we can't be clothed with three pieces of gowns to be taken to the ground for earthworms to eat. The soul will face its maker, whether we believe it or not. All through the Bible the Israelites were known to be God's children, yet when they were captured by their enemies, they always wanted to know something about them and their God because they lived in discontentment with their God.

Psalm 137:3 says, "For there those who carried us away asked for a song, and those who plundered us requested songs of joy saying sing to us one of the songs of Zion." When Samson was captured by the Philistines, they wanted to know the power of his strength. In Daniel 2 when King Nebuchadnezzar had a horrible dream and wanted to know the interpretation, he became furious to the extent that he decided to kill all his wise men and astrologers. Daniel and his companions remained faithful to God and served Him with whatever freedom they had. They didn't cry and join the rest who thought it impossible to interpret the dream. They knew their God. They went to God in prayer, and God revealed the answer to them. Sometimes tough situations will test us to find out whether we truly know God and can sing songs of Zion. In the spirit of heaviness we are told to put on the garment of praise. But here by the rivers of Babylon they couldn't sing at all. They had already hung up their harps and given up. Sometimes when we disobey God and get ourselves into uncomfortable situations, the only voice we hear is "He will never forgive; He has given up on us completely." But our God is always ready to receive us; He is always there. Jeremiah said when he wrote Lamentations 3 that His mercies are new every morning. He is sitting at the mercy seat every morning, waiting to see how many of His children come boldly to the throne room of grace to plead for mercy. We don't even have to wait a second to ask for forgiveness since we don't know the time of His coming. Every day our living here must be a preparation. We can't sing the Lord's song in a strange land when we are not ready to repent.

If as a Christian you are living with someone to whom you are not married just because the person has promised to marry you, and if you attend the same church, go about your normal daily work, and think God will understand because you've been together for so long, the answer is no. God will not understand any sin unless we repent from it.

King Nebuchadnezzar was requesting an interpretation, so they called all the astrologers and wise men, of which Daniel was one, and said if they couldn't answer satisfactorily, they would be killed. But Daniel knew his God, so he didn't panic. They went to the Lord in prayer, and the God who knows all secrets was able to reveal it to them. The Levites offer praises and worship to God and as such open the floodgates of heaven unto our earthly gathering, so everyone who holds a microphone in every worship service is important and should be holy.

We should study hymns like this one: "Take my life and let it be, / Consecrated, Lord, to thee. / Take my moments and my days, / Let them flow in ceaseless praise."

If you study the rest of the stanzas of this hymn, you will realize that it is filled with the words *let* and *take*. That is because God should get everything we own—everything. That means a consecrated life, a Spirit-filled life, a heavenly life, a life of ceaseless praise. Whether we are alone with God or in front of people, at work or at home, or out and about, our mouths should continually be filled with praises. When we hear that someone has taken someone else's life, in earthly language it means that he has murdered him or her. Here the songwriter is asking the Holy Spirit to take over and kill the flesh of self, but we have to take the initiative and offer ourselves because the Lord stands at the door knocking. We always say "wonderful Jesus, so gentle and pure," but a time is coming when we will witness His fierceness, so let us honor and serve Him faithfully. There are people with melodious voices placed as worship leaders who sing worldly songs, but as a worship leader your mouth should always produce ceaseless praise. You can't have it in both ways, so choose whom you want to glorify because the third stanza of the hymn goes like this: "Take my voice and let me sing / Always, only for my King. / Take my lips and let them be / Filled with messages from thee." As we offer ourselves, the Holy Spirit feeds us with songs that contain messages to glorify God. Some of the gospel songs we hear are humanly centered. We must be prayerful about that because in this hymn, the songwriter is willing to sing only to glorify the king. Any song that does not glorify the king is not of God. One preacher said we cannot sing songs that we do not obey, because it is just like preaching what we don't believe. So let's wait patiently on God to give us a song, a song that brings deliverance to the church and also adoration to our king, for we cannot sing the Lord's song in a strange land. Once, I was worshipping the Lord in this song:

> Crown him with many crowns
> The lamb upon his throne
> Hark, how the heavenly anthem
> Drowns all music but its own
> Awake my soul and sing
> Of Him who died for thee,
> And hail him as thy matchless King
> Through all eternity

As I kept on singing and repeating only the first stanza because that is what I remembered, I heard the Holy Spirit whispering these words in my soul:

> Awake your soul to sing
> For me alone your king
> Only one song that angels sing
> A song of Jesus Christ

The Lord opened my understanding that angels also sing Christ-centered songs. That is the heavenly anthem song, a song that enthrones our matchless king. That means there are certain types of songs that, when sung on earth, alert the angels to open the floodgates of heaven, backing us up on earth with heavenly instruments as we get in tune with the Holy Spirit. Beloved, we cannot sing any song just because it was launched by our favorite artist. Please, if the song does not glorify our king and does not point us to our final home, let's drop it. I don't think angels are singing with us the songs we are singing these days. Please understand me: many songs point to Jesus without naming Him in it. We should minimize songs that point to us; that is the nature of all worldly music. We are royalty in an everlasting kingdom, so we should not sing strange songs that do not agree with our spirit. There are also believers who buy worldly music and even dance to it. Please, we can't have it both ways. Let's choose whom we want to serve so that we will know what kind of song we can sing for Him. It's about time we experience His total anointing to prepare us for the coming kingdom, the New Jerusalem, our final home.

CHAPTER 9

A BRIDE ADORNED FOR HER HUSBAND

※

The book of Revelation is not an interesting book for the modern-day Christian.

Revelation: An act of revealing or communicating divine truth or an enlightening, astonishing disclosure. The book of Revelation is like a compact disc that summarizes the whole truth of the end of things and the beginning of the new life hereafter. It is true that the Bible is a treasure and God through His manifold wisdom granted that man would not be lost and be by himself or die without knowing the truth but receive everlasting life, yet few find it.

"Behold I am coming quickly, blessed is he who keeps the words of the prophecy of this book" (Revelation 22:7). The problem with the church is that we don't keep the Word of God richly in our hearts as we should. Our spiritual growth doesn't depend on how much we hear but on how we keep and walk in what we hear. Faith comes by hearing and hearing by the Word of God. Also faith without works is dead, and without faith it is impossible to please God. The Bible clearly declares these truths. The coming of the Lord is approaching, but there are many who are not prepared. Many things are happening around us concerning the prophecy of the coming of the Lord. In the Middle East the war between the Palestinians and the Israelites is clearly unfolding prophecy each day.

"Behold I will make Jerusalem a cup of drunkenness to all the surrounding) peoples when they lay siege against Judah and Jerusalem" (Zechariah 12:2). The terror that the whole world is facing now is because of Israel and anyone who is not a Muslim. These are some Quran verses, such as Surah 5:51, which says, "O you who believe do not take the Jew and the Christians for friends they are friend of each other and whoever among you to take them for a friend, then surely he is one of them. Allah does not guide these unjust people."

Surah 4:56 says, "Indeed, those who disbelieve in our verses - We will drive them into a Fire. Every time their skins are roasted through we will replace them with other skins so they may taste the punishment. Indeed, Allah is ever exalted in Might and Wise."
I believe that this information is necessary for our knowledge to study and understand prophecy, so that when we see and hear what is going on, we will not fear. They are preaching what the Quran is teaching them, and they are fulfilling their prophecy. No one is safe now. The world is not going to be the same again. Many people are terrified to travel. Church, let's wake up: the warfare has already begun, and we have more to do in the spiritual realm. In the physical realm there is a war between good and evil, and we can no longer ignore prophecy. It's about time the church started praying for Jerusalem and stopped criticizing its people, for they are our father's children as the Quran mentioned.

"And it shall come to pass in all the land says the Lord those two thirds in it shall be cut off and die, but one third will be left in it. I will bring the one third through the fire and it will refine them as silver is refined and test them as gold is tested, they will call my name and I will answer them and I will say, this is my people and each one will say this is my God" (Zechariah 13:8–9). Beloved brethren in the prophecy of

Zechariah, God is not looking for religious people to be called bride. The Bible is a book of preparation for people who are waiting to be a bride for Christ and to dwell with Him in His everlasting kingdom. This is another process that God wants His bride to go through. After two-thirds have died without Christ, we need massive evangelism because Christ needs to be proclaimed at all cost. The one-third left will have to go through a refinery process. Beloved, the time is short for us to engage in anything that doesn't count for His coming.

Earthly Bride, Her Preparation

There is a big preparation for a king's wedding; the rich and famous have to consult a bridal specialist because it's an event that you want to go well no matter what. People consult their bankers for a big loan. Sometimes the preparation begins even before the date is set. A child of God goes for biblical counseling and advice as part of the preparation. Most preparations are done by the bride once the man has proposed. The banquet hall needs to be decorated, and the bridal gown needs to be ready and fitted for the memorable occasion. Time will be spent on fasting and prayers because one wouldn't want anything to go wrong on that day. In giving out invitations, one has to be sure no friend or relative is left out. The day approaches with the excitement, the joy, the change of name, and finally the moment you meet your bridegroom intimately for the first time where you share all things in common. Yet the Bible says all this can't be compared with our meeting with the Lord.

Queen Esther didn't take meeting the king lightly, although they were already married. On this occasion it was really a life-and-death situation. She had already prepared before approaching the king for the sake of Israel. She had come in to save the people from death. In

Revelation 1 John saw Jesus with the appearance of a garment down to His feet and a golden sash girded around His chest. His head and hair were as white as wool and snow, His eyes were like a flame of fire, His feet were fine like brass refined in fire, His voice was like that of many waters, and His countenance was like the sun shining in all its brilliance. There and then John fell to his face as one who was dead. John was in the spirit yet when he came face-to-face with the King of Kings and the Lord of Lords, he couldn't stand His presence. The Lord had to touch him for him to hear what the Lord had to say because this message was the final warning to the church, and if we didn't take the Word of God seriously from Genesis, then Revelation should get our attention. The appearance John saw and described can't be seen with human eyes. The Lord told Moses that no one could see Him and live. If we claim to know Him and still want to have things our own way, we are missing our inheritance and the whole meaning of salvation package, which includes our going home to be with Him in the New Jerusalem. A hand and a head looking white as snow, a golden belt, brass feet, a flaming eye, and a voice that thunders is what is waiting for us, so with this in mind, how prepared should such a bride be to meet her groom. A garment down to His feet means the Lord has long been ready for His bride.

The First Heaven and the First Earth

John saw the first heaven and the first earth being passed away—not only the first earth but the first heaven also. The heaven above us is passing away, clearing His creation just to give way to the holy city. If we look around us, we realize that everything we see is passing away—the earth and the heavens, the sea and the mountains that He used seven days to create. The whole world is passing away for the New

Jerusalem. His tabernacle will soon take away the principalities and powers operating in the heavenly places, and the sea will be no more. That is why the enemy is fighting so hard to discourage us and make it look like all these preparations for this New Jerusalem is a fairy tale. The bride of Christ should not strive for it but rather try to live by the kingdom principles. Christ wants us to enjoy the fullness of life here, but as a bride we shouldn't forget to wear our combat boots also. It should remind us that the heavens and the earth are also passing away, and so are our mansions and properties. We should not be caught up in this world and its vanities, because something beyond our imagination is waiting for us.

The Rejoicing and True Bride

"Let us be glad and rejoice and give Him glory for the marriage of the lamb has come and His wife has made herself ready" (Revelation 19:7). In the midst of all the trials and tribulation this world is going to go through, the true believers will still rejoice and give God the glory because the bride is always ready, and nothing in this life matters any more. She can't even wait for the day. She will keep telling people about this event. Every day she will wake up with a joyful heart and a prepared mood because the groom may come anytime and the everlasting joy will begin. By singing inspirational songs like:

> Jerusalem my happy home,
> When shall I come to you?
> When shall my sorrows have an end?
> Your joys when shall I see?

A prepared mind and a ready heart will always flow with ceaseless praise regardless of the evil events around us. Most of us will not physically see the rapture but rather will wake up from the sleep of death to be caught up to meet Him in the air, so we should be ready each day to give our best worship and praise to Him. Let the Lord know how much you love Him every day because you don't know the day or year of your departure from this earth, and meet Him with joy. I once heard the story of a man visiting his brain dead wife in the intensive care unit of a hospital. He went there every day, and one time one of the staff working there told him to skip the next day and the rest. After all, his wife didn't know what was going on around her, and even if she came back to life, she wouldn't recognize him. The man's response was "I know all that, but I just want to fulfill my part of the marriage vow we took." We can't rely on our feelings any longer. Every day we draw closer to His coming and our departure from this life, so let us live prepared for Him. As we wake up every day and prepare to go to work or do whatever we do, let us prepare for Him. It may happen that, that day is our last day on earth.

"For since the beginning of the world men have not heard nor perceived by the ear, nor has the eye seen any God beside you, who acts for the one who waits for Him" (Isaiah 64:4).

God acts for those who wait for Him in service and in preparation for His coming. If our hearts are not set on pilgrimage, we can't render any service to Him, because the purpose of the new covenant is to prepare His chosen for the new heaven, the holy city. The Lord's purpose is to restore the lost paradise and prepare His chosen people as He chose Jerusalem on earth as His land, Israel. As any good waiter gets a good tip, so God will also in these last days act for any mind and heart that has prepared for His coming. Also rejoice, for many hearts are growing cold because of lawlessness. Sometimes the unseen things God does for us are more than what we see with our naked eyes. Our God is always waiting for us even if we don't yearn for Him. If we don't allow faith to establish God's Word in our hearts, we will miss the whole joy of our salvation.

The Acts of God Toward the Bride

The acts of God are all based on His loving kindness to His children. "But Jesus answered them my father has been working until now and I have been working" (John 5:17).

Ever since the fall of man God the father has acted everything out to restore the lost paradise. Jesus came to continue His father's work by doing good to mankind, but the Jewish elders had a problem with Him because He healed on the Sabbath day. Our God is not dead; He is alive and taking note of everything going on under the sun, especially with His righteous ones, so He can hear their cries and send angels to their rescue. All His acts and His ways have been demonstrated in the Bible. His son came to look for the bride for His new kingdom; He died to redeem us and didn't leave His bride comfortless but promised us the Holy Spirit to comfort us. As we have been sealed by His promise, we must continue to wait faithfully, and soon and very soon He will fulfill His final promise.

The Bride and the Spirit

When we received Jesus Christ as our Savior, we received a spiritual birth into the kingdom of God. Ephesians 1:3 tells us that we are sealed with the Holy Spirit of promise, and it continues to explain that the infilling of the Holy Spirit is a witness that we are a purchased possession of God to be revealed at His coming glory, so the Holy Spirit will live in us as a permanent resident, helping us in our preparation to meet God.

"And there are three that bear witness on earth the spirit, the water and the blood and these three agree as one" (1 John 5:8). The blood of Jesus redeemed us. This happened when the blood and water poured out from His side on the cross. The blessed Holy Spirit also seals us in Him as His possession so we have become the true children of God as the blood, water, and spirit agree that we are truly born again to Him by His Spirit. At the day of Pentecost the Holy Spirit was poured unto us just as Christ promised to lead us into all truth that pertained to here and the world to come, which is our heavenly home.

"And the spirit and the bride say come and let him who hears say come and let him who thirst whoever desires let him take the water of life freely" (Revelation 22:17). Whenever we are ready for whatever we have prepared ourselves for, we become realistic in our anticipation for that particular thing. We don't know how long the Spirit has been waiting for the bride to be ready so as to send the bridegroom, and those who have ears to hear what the Spirit is saying will also say, "Come." Those who are thirsty to drink with Him in His kingdom will also say, "Come." The Lord keeps asking, "Is the bride ready?" He knows that the church will not pray for Him to come. We will pray for everything else except His coming. That is why He will come unannounced. If He has to wait for the invitation from the church, the marriage ceremony will never happen.

The things of this life have got the best of some of us. That is why we are not willing to die, and the Lord knows it. We don't even pray for the salvation of our loved ones and will die without witnessing their salvation, but the Lord knows His own. The Bible says only those who are thirsty and hunger shall be filled. If we are not thirsty for the water of life, a time is coming when nothing will satisfy us again, and thus we will fall into deception, so the Lord will cut short the time and come for the bride. As we see the signs of His coming, the church must wake up in a massive evangelism, and the life we lead in this life must be a daily preparation to meet Him. If we continue to say no one is perfect, then no one is going because He is coming to take a church without spot or wrinkle. So let's pray and together with the Spirit say, "Come, Lord Jesus." Oh what a day it will be. Let's say "Amen," for it will surely come to pass.

CHAPTER 10

JERUSALEM ABOVE, OUR FOREVER JOY

And I saw the New Jerusalem and a New
earth: for the first heaven and the first were
passed away and there was no more sea.
—Revelation 21:1

Revelation 1 says that when John first saw our Lord in such an unspeakable appearance to review what was ahead for this world and the innumerable revelations that he witnessed, he saw a new heaven and a new earth. The first one, which mankind lives on, has miraculously passed away. It has truly passed away with everything in it except those whose names were written in the Lamb's book of life, those who have served Jesus faithfully with their life and lifetime.

Of course a world without a sea will be something new for John or anyone because the sea is bigger than the land on which mankind dwells. In Psalm 122 King David also saw a vision of the New Jerusalem and said he was glad when they said to him, "Let us go into the house of the Lord." David was not satisfied with an earthly house of worship because he also described a city that was compacted, which means it was joined or packed together, closely and firmly united, and Specially designed for particular occasions. David was happy to see such a city and happy to be among those going to dwell there. No more sea. Why? Oh, we know why. There are many things that exist in the sea, according to Revelation 13. John also saw a beast rise up out of the sea, the sea has been his dwelling place, the sea will be no more, the beast and the dragon and all those demonic entities have made the sea their dwelling place, and most of the world's sewage systems drain their filth into the sea, so the New Jerusalem definitely cannot have this worldly sea anymore. The only sea that will be there is mentioned in Revelation 4:6 and Revelation 15:12: the glassy sea or a sea of glass is what he saw, a sea of stillness and tranquility.

Beloved, we have to go there to witness and enjoy all these blessed hopes. This New Jerusalem is a special, prepared city. It has been there for more than two thousand years, and is still in preparation. These days, no one wants to live in a village or small town. Most people prefer to live in a city because they will have access to a lot of things. Every village boy or girl dreams that one day he or she will live in a big city for a lifestyle change, to get a good job and raise their family. And so the New Jerusalem is a special adorned city prepared by the architect of the universe. Why is it that some believers are not crazy to lead a life that will grant them access to this holy and golden city? And why is it that the whole world is not seeking to go there? Because the things of this world has blinded their minds? Why will people in other countries sell their land and give up their goods and jobs to get to nations with big cities so they can fulfill their dreams? Well, for your information the biggest city is in preparation. You don't need any real estate agent to get you a building there no matter how rich you are. God's only begotten son, who died and shed His precious blood to redeem mankind from their sins, will take you there. If you really want to go, just accept Him and ask for forgiveness, and His Spirit will help you live for Him.

"They desire a better country that is Heavenly wherefore God is not Ashamed to be called their God for he hath repared for them a city" (Hebrews 11:16).

Many people and religions do not understand that Christianity is not a religion. It is Jesus Christ living His life through a human heart producing godly characteristics. That is why no born-again child of God with Christ in his or her heart will ever destroy his or her faith or commit suicide because He is always with us no matter how we feel. We are looking forward to being with Him in the New Jerusalem. That is why we can't hide our identity. There are some people who call themselves Christians and the only ones who knows it are themselves and God because of the double standards by which they are living. Neighbors, workmates, and even sometimes our spouses don't know we are Christians because the evidence of showing the good fruits is not there. But those who desire this new heavenly country are not ashamed of or afraid to talk about it everywhere they go, regardless of what people say or think about them because this is a blessed hope. Our real life is not the one we are living now. Our real life begins in this New Jerusalem, so this excitement and spiritual energy must be used to serve Him coupled with our life and everything we do.

The New Jerusalem, the City of Glory

"And 1 John saw the Holy city New Jerusalem, coming down from God out of Heaven, Prepared as a Bride adorned for her Husband" (Revelation 21:2).

The earthly bride must adorn herself for her husband and her audience, and the audience adorns themselves to suit the occasion, but her mind will definitely be on the husband to make sure the bridegroom is in place waiting for her. Adorning the bride takes time by the time she gets a hairdo, manicure, and pedicure, and has her makeup done. All her underwear is new, and her bridesmaids also must be adorned. All these preparations cost money and time. Some prayer and fast to smooth things, that say that even for earthly King Ahasuerus in Esther 2, with all his authority, choosing a bride was not a simple thing. It took twelve months of preparation and purifications for any maid who wanted to be the king's bride: six months with oil of myrrh, and six months of widely sweet odors. We have to know also that all these preparations were not for the bride but for the king.

So it is for us today. We should allow the Holy Spirit to really do a good work in us, bathing and anointing. Even an earthly king will not allow just any bride but one who is purified and anointed with sweet oil to be in his palace. How can we underestimate our preparation in this New Jerusalem to be with our bridegroom? Perhaps no other book in the Bible portrays this preparation in such detail as the book of Esther. This preparation is very important because we are going to a holy city. Yes, John saw a holy city, the New Jerusalem.

Every bride is beautiful in her wedding gown and adornments because that is the day she is saying yes to the husband. She has waited for him all her life and stands in front of the whole world, so she must look gorgeous regardless of how much it costs her. So dear beloved, it cost God His only begotten son to redeem and prepared for this New Jerusalem. It should encourage every believer who wants to go there to truly prepare our way of life to find such a city. There is a chorus by Paul Wilbur that goes like this:

> Shalom Shalom Jerusalem
> Peace be to you

When Messiah Come to take us home
May His praise be found in you.

When Messiah comes, whether by the rapture or our being called to eternal rest, may we go with a peaceful, forgiving, and loving heart. That's why the Bible warns us not to let the sun go down on our anger. It would be unwise to ignore such scriptures because we don't know when we are to depart, and we can't afford to soil our garment or be left behind, because the bridegroom will definitely inspect us. We are all going to appear before the judgment seat of Christ.

Our Robe of Righteousness
"So the servants went out into the streets and gathered all the people they could find, the bad as well as the good, and the wedding hall was filled with guests. But when the king came in to see the guests, he noticed a man there who was not wearing wedding clothes" (Matthew 22:10–11).

The man was unprepared for the wedding was shocked that the Lord would confront him to walk out because according to his own righteousness, his clothes were okay for a marriage dinner. Beloved, the condition of our heart is very important. Sometimes our hatred for one another can't be seen or heard in our speech, and many things we hide in our hearts are tearing our robes apart every day. We need to love one another, for love, patience, and endurance are all the fruits of the Holy Spirit. If we don't have them, how can we say we have a fellowship with the Spirit?

These days we hear a lot about the church and its problems. The devil is working hard, but thanks be to God that no matter what, the gates of hell cannot prevail against Christ's kingdom. It is the people to whom the kingdom belongs who need to take it by force with righteous living. The devil talks to us about one another. He can talk to you about your husband, your children, your wife, your boss, and everyone else. These thoughts are negative. Instead of us sending them to the Holy Ghost laboratory to find out the truth, we turn against one another and fight and tear our robes, so by the time we get to the dinner, we have no dinner garment. Please remember that we have to take negative thoughts captive. And that the mind of Christ is the mind that will take us to this holy city. All things are naked before God. Our hidden organ—our heart—is bare before God. We need to read the Word of God daily to cleanse and flush things that are not supposed to stick there, because we don't want to get to the gates and get the shock of our life. No one is getting away with anything. Let us stay focused on this heavenly vision, for that day we will not have anything to say. We can't preach or sing anymore but will face judgment. Our robes and garments will determine who we are. When people are going to a wedding, you can most of the time know for sure by the way they have dressed. People also wear different kinds of job uniforms. Some clergy also have different kinds according to their calling and office, but on this particular wedding, the right garment will be determined only by the bridegroom.

The Oil in Our Lamp; the Anointing

"They that were foolish took their Lamps, and took no oil with them: But the wise took oil in their vessel with their lamps" (Matthew 25:3–4) As believers in Jesus Christ who see prophecy unfolding toward the end time, we should be heavenly minded. Only the Spirit and the bride can be ready for the bridegroom. Our robe of righteousness and the Holy Spirit in our lives should walk hand in hand. There are so many things that drain our oil gradually, such as not reading the Word and not practicing what the Word says to us. The ten virgins seemed to have everything together until that midnight cry. This is our grace period when we can mend our ways and trim our lamps because when the trumpet sounds, it will be too late for anything. The danger is not realizing there is a shortage till that crucial time. This is one of the saddest stories or parables in the Bible. So always, let us check our fruits to see what is on our tree of life. If you know you are banana tree and you are bearing ginger and pepper, you quickly and immediately check your soil, which is your heart. When anger, uncontrollable lust, jealousy, or lack of love drains our oil and our access to this heavenly gate, it is our righteousness and holiness that will pave a way for us to be at this wedding feast, for it will be a great day. Jerusalem above will be our chief joy, and nothing there can be compared to our imagination unless we go there and see it for ourselves. Our Christian life should start to take shape to fit our heavenly home. What are our conversations and what are we talking about?

"But our citizenship is in heaven. And we eagerly await a Savior from there, the Lord Jesus Christ" (Philippians 3:20).

Is our conversation centered on our destination home? If we are interested as we are supposed to be, why are we not preaching and talking about it more? If a child has been told that one day his father will come and take him to where he is, there won't be a single day in which he does not tell his friends about it, because he will want to go where his father is; he loves his father and wants to be with him. So should be our conversations and all our doings as people who are seeking a heavenly home. One time I was preparing my home nicely for a visitor, making sure everything was in place, watching the time frequently to make sure I would be done by the time the doorbell rang. Suddenly the Lord spoke to me and said, "But my coming will be different." I laughed and said, "Yes, I know that, Lord," but it won't be a laughing matter that day.

The coming of our Lord is drawing nearer every minute and second, and the devil is still waging war with our minds, but we must know that we are in serious warfare and dealing with all kinds of different spirits even in the church. The same manner of dressing you see in nightclubs will be seen in the church, in addition to a whole lot of indications of our lifestyle that we are not supposed to portray. The church has lost its discipline; we have come short of our heavenly vision. We are always praying for new souls in the church, but we fail to discipline ourselves.

The tree of life was a symbol of the everlasting life that God has proposed to give to His children, so immediately they ate this fruit of wisdom and knowledge. They saw a flaming sword to guide this tree of life and prevent them from touching it. This tree of life in Revelation 22:2 is in the middle of the street that leads to the gate of the holy city. It will bear fruits every month, and its leaves will heal and finally wipe away the final curse that God imposed upon man after the fall in the garden. Revelation 22:14 tells us that blessed are those who do His commandments, that they may have the righteousness to the tree of life and enter through the gates of the city. When we do His commandments, we are blessed right here on earth. The one whose heart is set on God will quickly resolve issues because he is not living to himself but has crucified himself with Christ for the life that he lives. We can get access to His gate by obeying His commandments, but before we get to the gate, we have to get to the tree of life.

The Tree of Life

It is this same tree of life that the Lord planted in the garden of Eden in Genesis 2:13 together with the forbidden tree of wisdom and knowledge. Man disobeyed God by listening to the deceiver to eat the fruit and be like God; meanwhile the Lord told them not to eat because when they eat it, they would die. The enemy is still in the lying business, always whispering in our ears, and forcing negative thoughts in our minds to depress us.

Die to Self and Live in the Kingdom

The Bible clearly says that flesh and blood cannot inherit the kingdom of God; therefore with our fleshly nature it is impossible to experience the joy of the Lord.

Romans 14:17 says, "For the kingdom is not eating and drinking, but righteous, peace, and joy in the Holy Spirit."

The godly joy comes only when we operate in the Holy Spirit by doing and obeying the Lord of Lords even when it hurts, when people laugh at and ridicule us. That's how we're to live in the Spirit because the Word is Christ in us. We shouldn't dare to speak and pray in tongues and live contrary to the Word of God. That's not the definition of a Spirit-filled believer, for we are the bride of Christ.

We bring problems to ourselves when we allow the enemy to infiltrate our minds and souls with negative thoughts. Most of the time our hope in Christ also helps us live comfortably here in this life, and by so doing, we lose focus on our final destination, the things He has taken thousands of years to prepare for us, and we get disappointed and lose faith.

I used to live like that and most of the time lost the true joy until He touched me and changed my thought patterns.

When we compare ourselves with one another instead of Christ, we miss our chief joy. He being our Lord set a joy before him, a kind of joy that moved him to die a painful and shameful death on the cross to bring many souls into this New Jerusalem, sitting at the right hand of the father. Our Lord Jesus Christ with His disciples, as He started His ministry, had one focus. So should we. He didn't have to associate Himself with things of this life.

"For the Lord Himself will descend from Heaven with a shout, with the voice of an archangel, and with the trumpet of God. And the dead in Christ will rise first then we who are alive and remain shall be caught up together with them in the clouds to meet the Lord in the air. And thus we shall always be with the Lord" (1 Thessalonians 4:17–18)

So, dear believer in Christ, don't be in sorrow anymore, for our final destination will be with the Lord in the New Jerusalem. Amen.

END-TIME CHART

About the Jews, Israel, and Jerusalem

Genesis 12:3 and 15:18

Ezekiel 20:36, 37, 38–39

Revelation 7 and 12:2

Zechariah 14

Daniel 12:11–12

Joel 3

About a Great Tribulation

Daniel 12:1

Revelation 12:11

Matthew 24:21

About the Beast, False Prophet, Satan, "666"

Revelation 6:16, 11, 13–18 and 19:20

Revelation 20:1–6 and 20:7–15

What Jesus Taught

Matthew 24

Mark 13

Luke 21

About the Nations, Antichrist, Armageddon

1 John 2:18

2 John 7

Daniel 7

Revelation 16:13–21 and 19:11–21

Daniel 11:36–45

Joel 3:2–21

Zechariah 14:12

About the New Heaven and New Earth

Revelation 21 and 22

Isaiah 65:17

Phone number: 718-930-7842

Printed in the United States
By Bookmasters